GOD ON
OUR SIDE

*The British Padres in
World War I*

GOD ON
OUR SIDE

Edited by
Michael Moynihan

A LEO COOPER BOOK
SECKER & WARBURG · LONDON

First published in Great Britain 1983 by
Leo Cooper in association with
Martin Secker & Warburg Limited
54 Poland Street, London W1V 3DF.

Copyright for introduction and linking passages.
© 1983 Michael Moynihan

ISBN 0-436-29402-8

The author is grateful to Mr Harold Spooner, Mr David
Railton, Mr Maurice Murray, Mr Victor Tanner and Mr
Willie Doyle for permission to reprint material included
in the book which has been so kindly supplied by the
Imperial War Museum.

Photoset in Great Britain by
Rowland Phototypesetting Limited, Bury St Edmunds, Suffolk
and printed by St Edmundsbury Press
Bury St Edmunds, Suffolk

CONTENTS

ACKNOWLEDGEMENTS

I AM INDEBTED to the Imperial War Museum for access to their archives. In particular I would like to thank Mr Roderick Suddaby, Head of the Department of Documents, for assistance in selecting material, and the Reading Room staff for help with research.

For valuable background information I am greatly obliged to Mr A. P. Spooner, MBE, Mr A. S. Railton, Mr Mark Thomas, Mrs Joan Roberts and Mr E. J. Watson.

A mine of information on Anglican padres and religious attitudes generally has been Alan Wilkinson's *The Church of England and the First World War* (SPCK 1978), and I am also indebted to Cassells and the estate of the late Ernest Raymond for the use of excerpts from *Tell England*.

PREFACE

FLYING LOW OVER a quiet sector of the Western Front one Sunday in 1915, a French pilot descried two religious services in progress on either side of no-man's-land. The two altars, the two padres, the two groups of soldier worshippers, seemed reflections of each other—'so exactly alike that it looked silly'.

The pilot was the novelist Henri Barbusse and his description of this bizarre spectacle comes in his 1916 classic, *Le Feu*, which was published in English in 1917 under the title *Under Fire*. Barbusse goes on to relate how he flew lower to investigate:

> Then I could hear. I heard one murmur, one only. I could only gather a single chant that passed by me on its way to heaven. I got some shrapnel just at the moment when, very low down, I made out two voices from the earth that made up one—'Gott mit uns!' and 'God is with us!'—and I flew away. What must the good God think about it all?

'God on our side', was the confident claim of every protagonist in the First World War. Nowhere more so than in England. Scarcely had war been declared than, from pulpits and platforms up and down the land, the God of Battles was being invoked. The war was depicted as a Holy Crusade, the Kaiser as the anti-Christ ('Nailed Hand against Mailed Fist'). And, to the strains of 'Onward Christian soldiers' and 'Fight the good fight', with a Union Jack for altar cloth, the padre made his bow on the parade ground.

Though chaplains had appeared on the payroll of the English Army as early as the reign of Edward I, in the thirteenth century, never before had so many clergy, of so many denominations, donned uniform to provide spiritual succour to the troops. The number had risen from 117 at the outbreak of the war in August 1914 to 3,475 by the armistice in November 1918. Of these 1,985 were Church of England, 649 Roman Catholic, 303 Presbyterean, 256 Wesleyan, 251 United Board (Baptists, Congregationalists, Primitive Methodists and United Methodists), 16 Jewish, 10 Welsh Calvanists and 5 Salvation Army. Of the 172 padres who lost their lives, 88 were Anglican. Four padres were awarded the Victoria Cross, and many more received other decorations or commendations for bravery.

In memoirs and popular histories of the war the padre has been mostly ignored. Where mentioned at all, it has usually been in dismissive, even derogatory, terms. This book provides a unique close-up of the padre in action—and of his impact on the Tommy. It is based on the diaries and letters of six padres (five Anglican, one Roman Catholic) who served on the Western Front, in Mesopotamia and at Gallipoli. With one exception, the manuscripts have only recently come to light, donated to the Imperial War Museum after the death of their authors. They have been chosen from a number of similar first-hand accounts (all by Anglican padres) as best depicting the experiences of padres who shared enough of the horrors of trench warfare to have their own faith severely tested.

The most quoted allusion to the padre's standing among troops at the front appears in Robert Graves' classic memoir,

Goodbye to All That (first published in 1929 and still widely read) and is here worth giving at length as a yard-stick.

. . . For Anglican regimental chaplains we had little respect. If they had shown one-tenth the courage, endurance and other human qualities that the regimental doctor showed, the British Expeditionary Force might well have started a religious revival. But they had not, being under orders to avoid getting mixed up with the fighting and to stay behind with the transport. Soldiers could hardly respect a chaplain who obeyed these orders, and yet not one in fifty seemed sorry to obey them. Occasionally, on a quiet day in a quiet sector, the chaplain would make a daring afternoon visit to the support line and distribute a few cigarettes, before hurrying back. But he was always much to the fore in rest-billets. Sometimes the Colonel would summon him to come up with the rations and bury the day's dead; he would arrive, speak his lines, and shoot off again.

The position was complicated by the respect that most commanding officers had for the cloth—though not all. The Colonel in one battalion I served with got rid of four new Anglican chaplains in four months; finally he applied for a Roman Catholic, alleging a change of faith in the men under his command. For the Roman Catholic chaplains were not only permitted to visit posts of danger, but definitely enjoined to be wherever fighting was, so that they could give extreme unction to the dying. And we had never heard of one who failed to do all that was expected of him and more . . .

Even accepting that Graves, invalided home early in 1917, missed the final stages of the war when Anglican padres were actively encouraged to go up the line, the picture he has implanted of them as effete camp followers, lacking in courage and 'remarkably out of touch with their troops', is scarcely borne out by the accounts that follow. Though Graves' testimony to the courage of Roman Catholic padres is amply justified in the case of the remarkable Father Doyle portrayed in Chapter 6, there is no doubting the readiness of these Anglicans to risk their lives, or of their desire (as one puts it) 'to be with the men at this their time of deepest need'.

How representative are these self-portraits it is impossible to gauge from the sparse information available. But from the only comprehensive survey of the work of Anglican padres at the front, in Alan Wilkinson's scholarly *The Church of England and the First World War* (published in 1978 by the Society for Promoting Christian Knowledge), it would seem that there were many Anglican padres equally dedicated —and equally frustrated. For if there is a common denominator in these variegated accounts it is a feeling of inadequacy in face of widespread fatalism, side by side with an awed recognition of the 'Christ-like' qualities that flourished in the trenches without benefit of any belief in 'God on our side'. From hindsight the First World War padres can be seen as spearheading a hoped-for religious revival that failed to materialise, and a brief summary of the social and emotional climate of the times may help to put the issues into historic perspective.

At the outset of the war England (as Great Britain was commonly known) was the envy of the world, hub of the greatest empire in history, and its social structure had only begun to be threatened by such rebellious spirits as the trade unions and the suffragettes. Religious observance had never been more flourishing, with an estimated 30 million nominal members of the Church of England. Among the middle classes churchgoing was an accepted weekly ritual. Even upper-class house parties in country mansions took attendance at Sunday matins as part of the hospitality. It was among the industrial working class that religion counted least (and at which the 'revival' was chiefly aimed). Among the still-numerous agricultural workers, Sunday chapel-going was the great community occasion, an oasis in lives of grinding labour and poverty. The lusty singing of Tommies on the march, often to ribald verses set to familiar hymn tunes, was a safety-valve at the front as it had been at home.

What was to be devastatingly revealed during the war was that much of this religious observance had no deeper roots than social convention or escapism. At home such factors as the break-up of the family, the introduction of Sunday labour and the abandonment of accepted standards of behaviour lastingly depleted the church congregations. At the front something far more cataclysmic undermined the consolations of religion. With death in its most hideous forms all around, it needed a faith founded on rock to sustain any belief in a 'merciful Father'.

Yet it was with the assumption of a nation united under God that the churches rallied to the bugle call at the start of the war. Though there were a few bravely dissentient voices against the rising tide of hatred against the Hun, it was forgotten that this was a war of Protestant England (allied with Catholic France) against Protestant Germany, cradle of the Reformation. Forgotten, too, were the ecumenical links between the two countries that had been forged in recent years, highlighted by a reciprocal visit to Germany, in 1906, by an interdenominational delegation from Britain (including a number of Anglican bishops), where they had been warmly welcomed at a conference in Potsdam by the Kaiser himself.

The extent to which patriotism could distort the Christian ethos is chillingly indicated in a sermon preached by the Bishop of London, Bishop Winnington-Ingram, in Westminster Abbey after a year of war. In it he called upon the nation's manhood to

band in a great crusade—we cannot deny it—to kill

Germans. To kill them, not for the sake of killing, but to save the world; to kill the good as well as the bad; to kill the young men as well as the old, to kill those who have showed kindness to our wounded as well as those fiends who crucified the Canadian sergeant, who superintended the Armenian massacres, who sank the Lusitania—and to kill them lest the civilisation of the world should itself be killed . . .

From all accounts it was the padres who assumed a similar tone of bellicosity in their confrontations with the troops at the front who did most to discredit the religion they espoused. The more sensitive became quickly aware that the hysteria and jingoism of the home front had no place on the battlefield. In an impersonal war of attrition the enemy in their trenches across no-man's-land appeared rather as fellow-victims than fiends. The atrocity stories of the popular press were discounted. Though superstitions were prevalent, derision greeted such accounts of supernatural intervention as the 'Angels of Mons'. Widely accepted at home as visible evidence that God was on our side, this reputed vision of angels appearing above the battlefield and safeguarding the British withdrawal from Mons in the first month of the war, had, in fact, originated from a fictional short story in the London *Evening News* (in which the 'long line of shapes, with a shining about them' had been, not angels, but the ghosts of Agincourt bowmen).

The last chapter of this book, which is devoted to the attitudes towards religion of the fighting troops, makes it clear that fatalism was the predominant mood at the front ('If it's got your bloody number on it there's nothing you can do about it'). What can never be known is to what extent men driven to extremes of fear and suffering found within them a 'last resort' belief in a personalised God. A regular army Tommy, whose collection of letters from the front is one of

the War Museum's rarest acquisitions, may have been revealing as much as can be known when he wrote to his
sweetheart:

> Well Ivy you say that you pray for me every night and I
> thank you for it. I know a lot of men here before the war
> were great sinners but I know that they often pray now, it
> is the time the Germans are shelling our trenches that they
> think there is a God. I am not saying that I said my
> prayers before the war, because I did not, but I don't
> believe I have missed a night since I have been out here
> and ever since the Battle of Neuve Chapelle I have
> believed there is a God because I prayed to Him before the
> battle to keep me safe and He did, I had some marvellous
> escapes . . .

Were the 'moments of religious awareness' mentioned by
C. E. Montague (Chapter 3) as widespread as he suggests?
Could they have been fanned, by a different breed of padre,
into the religious revival even the agnostic Robert Graves
could envisage? Or were these no more than a passing cry in
the dark, the kind of last throw of the dice indicated in Padre
Spooner's account of the siege of Kut (Chapter 1), when it
was not until the final stage of the prolonged agony that the
Garrison Commander called for special prayers for divine
intervention and Spooner wrote in his diary: 'I do not think
hymns have ever been sung or prayers made with greater
earnestness'?

What is certain is that, with some nine million men in
uniform killed (over three quarters of a million British),
Britain emerged from the war in a very different climate of
belief than at the outset. The war's traumatic effect on the
human psyche was summed up by Bishop William Wand,
Bishop of London (who had himself served as a padre), in
Promise of Greatness, published in 1968 as a memorial volume
for the 50th anniversary of the Armistice. His conclusion

would surely have seemed beyond the bounds of possibility to Wand's firebrand predecessor Bishop Winnington-Ingram, as he trumpeted his clarion call to kill, kill, kill in the name of the God of Battles.

In general we may say that the most important religious effect of the war was to produce throughout mankind a new habit of mind. Whereas hitherto the majority had looked at least nominally beyond space and time for its incentives and rewards, now the outlook became frankly this-worldly. Man himself, rather than his gods, became the measure of all things.

CHAPTER ONE

FAITH
UNDER SIEGE

O N 15 APRIL 1916, in the besieged fortress town of
Kut-al-Amara on the banks of the Tigris in Mesopotamia, the Reverend Harold Spooner, Anglican padre with an
expeditionary force of the Indian Army, received an urgent
request from Major-General Charles Townshend, the
Commanding Officer, that special prayers be said for prolonged fine weather. Unless the rain and wind abated, and
the swollen river subsided, the relief force, making its third
attempt to break through the encircling Turkish army, could
not hope to succeed.

Rarely could British troops have been more sorely in need
of divine intervention. After 134 days of siege (the longest in
our military history) Tommies and Sepoys were dying of
starvation, while the death role from shellfire and snipers'
bullets continued to mount. Most of the garrison's horses
and mules had been eaten and the bread ration had been
reduced to four ounces a day. Men were driven to assuage
their hunger with the meat of dogs, cats, hedgehogs, spar-
rows, starlings.

After receiving the General's request [Spooner records in
his diary] I went into the Chapel alone and prayed to
God. When I came out the clouds were beginning to thin
and the sun to break through. Shortly, too, the wind

began to veer to the North—a sure sign of fine weather. Thank GOD for this—it is our only chance of being relieved.

Spooner's jubilation was short-lived. Prolonged fine weather did not ensue. God, it must have seemed, was moving in a mysterious way. It was the Turks who had cause to praise Allah. Two weeks later Townshend was forced to surrender, and some 12,000 emaciated British and Indian troops were rounded up for a 1,200-mile forced march across the scorching desert towards a brutal captivity only the toughest were to survive.

Rarely can the God of Battles have appeared so two-faced as in this epic siege, one of the grimmest but least celebrated confrontations in the First World War. While Spooner and his two fellow padres (Roman Catholic and Wesleyan) strove indefatigably throughout the siege to keep faith in the Christians' God alive, the Turks were invoking with equal confidence their Mohammedan God. Bundles of pamphlets thrown into the British trenches, calling on the Indian troops to murder their English officers and desert to the Sultan, were missives in a holy crusade. 'Oh dear Indian Brother,' the pamphlet began, 'You understand the fact well that God has created this war for setting India free from the hands of the cruel English . . .' Later the inhuman treatment of their captives was justified as retribution for the sins of the hitherto all-powerful British Raj.

Spooner's voluminous diary of the siege and its aftermath is a remarkable testimony to the buoyancy of his own faith. After the war, as a direct result of his protracted ordeal, he was to spend 16 years in a nursing home in a state of mental collapse, unable even to recognise his wife and two sons. But little of the anguished strain that was building up registers in the diary. Concern for others is uppermost.

Born in 1880, the son of a clergyman, Spooner took orders

at Salisbury Theological College and went to India in 1911. As Garrison Chaplain to the Middlesex Regiment, he entered fully into the life of the regiment. A small, wiry man, still a bachelor, a keen sportsman (he played polo for the regiment), with an engaging, down-to-earth manner, he was an obvious choice as a padre in the field. In 1915 he joined the expeditionary force in Mesopotamia, where they had been sent in November 1914 with the object of protecting the Royal Navy's oil supply in the Persian Gulf.

The siege of Kut was the outcome of a rash attempt to capture Baghdad by a division of the expeditionary force under General Townshend. Although capturing the stronghold of Ctesiphon 15 miles from Baghdad (with heavy losses), the division was forced to retreat on Kut when the Turks produced two fresh divisions. It was during this retreat that Spooner volunteered to stay with a party of wounded, displaying a courage that earned him the Military Cross. A diary kept by one of the wounded (who later described him as 'our incomparable padre') gives this picture of him:

Six of us were in the trench, under a tremendous rifle fire with bullets whizzing over and thudding into the parapet. Padre Spooner was busy making a white flag in case it should be needed, for there was nothing else for it as we were all helpless cases. He then proceeded to stand on the parapet under heavy fire and give us the news, just as if he were on the stand at a Race Meeting and we down in the crowd below. The last piece of news I remember was: 'They're only 300 yards away, but it's all right, we're giving them H-ll!' They got no further.

Later the wounded were loaded on mule-drawn carts and Spooner led the way on foot. 'All through the last 3 days he has been with us,' the diary relates, 'looking after us, feeding us, and reassuring us with his cheerfulness and coolness, when things looked bad, and showing absolute disregard for his own safety. His is a splendid example . . .'

That example was to persist throughout the five-months'-long siege, from 7 December 1915 to 29 April 1916. Two hundred and fifty river-miles south of Baghdad, surrounded by desert, Kut was formerly the centre of a busy grain trade, with a mosque, a flourmill, two bazaars, a scattering of two-storey houses and gardens, but mostly a squalid maze of alleyways flanked by mud hovels with matting roofs. Now, to its densely packed Arab population of 6,000, were added some 10,000 British and Indian fighting men, 3,500 Indian non-combatants and 2,000 sick and wounded.

Spooner was later to record that the little room that served as his chapel in Kut was remarkable in that no shell penetrated it, though its outside walls were liberally spattered by enemy bullets. A total of 103 shells found their way into the British General Hospital, whose wards consisted of a double row of cubicles converted from the little shops on either side of the covered bazaar. But, though he stuck to a regular routine of chapel services and hospital visits, Spooner felt his presence to be quite as necessary in the front line trenches.

By the time the diary starts, 17 days after the commencement of the siege, the Turkish trenches had moved close to the town, after a series of savage attacks and counter-attacks and a remorseless bombardment by the Turkish artillery. The deaths, injuries and destruction caused by the constant shelling are a refrain throughout the siege section of Spooner's diary, which alone runs to over 35,000 words, and from which the extracts that follow can give only a representative impression.

Xmas Eve. Got up at 6.30. The enemy are attacking and rifle fire is furious, heavy guns terrific. All ready for service at 7.30 but had to wait until nearly 8 because of rattle of musketry—their bullets were hitting wall and ceiling and dust and dirt falling all over my Communion Table. Nine communicants. At 8.45 I got to the officers' ward when 4 Communicated. The noise was still pretty bad and while I walked to an inner room with a Chalice a bullet hit the door I was walking through.

At 10 a.m. I had breakfast and had a lively time dodging shells. At 11.30 one of the many shells which burst in the courtyard set on fire some ammunition —fearful excitement—bullets were being hurled all over the shop—then a huge explosion which sent things sky high and this seemed to put the fire out . . .

I was going to tiffin when I saw the Norfolks marching out to reinforce the Fort. The Turks had forced their way into the redoubt, cutting the barbed wire. The time was critical. For the Turks to have made two determined attacks in broad daylight was unusual, and things looked pretty serious . . . Later we learnt the Turks had been driven back, leaving many dead, during a counter-attack by the Oxfords. We breathed again . . .

Christmas Day. 14 Communicants at 7.30 Celebration. All quiet, no shells or bullets. Had General Nur-a-Din the heart to leave us at peace on Christmas Day—or had we given the Turks too hot a grilling? The latter, I think. At 9 I started with my orderly for 2nd line trenches to hold H.C. in 'Dorset Redoubt'. The trenches were wonderful. Snipers occasionally had a shot. But what an extraordinary service. 18 officers and men in a dugout. A milk box for an Altar—my big wooden cross made by the Norfolks' Pioneers on top of it. A flask for Chalice —ordinary plate for patten—bullets whizzing overhead.

We sang two hymns—'While Shepherds watch their flocks' and 'Hark the Herald Angels sing.' Never have I heard such devout and earnest singing—never have I seen a congregation so thoughtful and devout. Were the Turks listening, I wonder, and did they understand? . . .

[23]

Coming back we had to cross an open space exposed to snipers—but we got through all right. I saw a dead Sikh who had only been buried a few inches deep—his face all exposed—horrible. At lunch John Clifton, A.D.C. to General Townshend, told us that the Turks' casualties yesterday were estimated at 800—that they were evidently spending the day in getting the wounded away. Many dead outside our trenches unable to be removed . . .

Took Evensong in Hospital at 6 p.m.—Such singing again! The dear old Xmas hymns. Officers from outside turned up—doctors and orderlies. A short address re Xmas and message of 'Peace'.

Sunday 26 December. Very quiet day. After morning Celebration I went with my orderly to try and find the Oxfords' trenches, to take a Service. We got into the wrong trenches and consequently sniped at pretty badly. Directly our topees showed above, a sniper had a shot at once, each time the bullet came unpleasantly near. Once I was foolish enough to put my head above the trench to see where we were—did not do it a second time. One hadn't realised the Turkish snipers were only a few hundred yards away . . .

28 December . . . Had tiffin with General Houghton in his dugout. He said that seeing the Padre in the trenches was 'as water in a thirsty land' . . .

30 December . . . Called on Father Mullen, R.C., and Rev. Wright, Wesleyan, who showed me 2 huge holes in the wall of their room made by the bursting of a 'Windy Lizzie'. They certainly had a marvellous escape. Five bodies awaited burial—but the shell fire is so heavy that we must wait for a bit, until things are quieter . . .

A Turk came up to the Fort with a white flag and Colonel Brown (O.C. Fort) allowed them a few hours to take away their dead and wounded—so for a short while

Turks, British and Indians were all out of their trenches walking about. Then the order came that they must return to their trenches, and so they did . . .

1 January 1916. Had an early breakfast and went to the trenches to hold a Communion Service for the West Kents and 1/4 Hants. About 20 Communicants—mostly officers. We sang 2 Christmas hymns. It all seemed to mean a great deal to these men facing death daily—sometimes hourly. I then talked to many of the soldiers in the trenches who seemed very cheery and in no way depressed . . .

3 January. Got up early and went down the trenches with my orderly to the Fort to Celebrate the Holy Communion as a special message had been sent by General Houghton. He met me and escorted me down. We talked of the war and the good it was doing to Men's Characters.

'Padre', he said, 'I do not know whether it was a coincidence or what, but during our retreat from Ctesiphon, just as the order had been given and we were all feeling as depressed as we could be, that nothing could ever go right again, and that all was up with us, I walked along one of the trenches and saw a small Prayer Book lying on the parapet. I picked it up and it was opened at the hymn 540, "Fight the Good Fight"—Fight the good fight of faith—lay hold on Eternal life. Call it a coincidence if you like but all I can tell you is nothing else has mattered to me ever since, come what may.' Thus it is that things happen to one at the front . . .

10 January . . . I have now had shrapnel through my pants, a bullet through my boot, my horse shot. The amusing thing is I was wearing neither pants nor boots, nor was I riding my pony when he was shot . . .

15 January . . . Saw a terrible crowd of Arab women shrieking round the body of a woman who had just been

shot by a sniper while going down to fetch water from the river. These women will not take the covered way and this is the result. One realised what the Eastern wailing at the death of a relative meant . . .

21 January. Rain! Rain! Rain! River rising, trenches full of water, troops up to their waists, and still rain comes. It is very very serious. The 1st line had to be evacuated, and while doing this there were many casualties—the rush of water was so sudden that there was nothing to do but to jump onto the parapet and so into the open and exposed to the Turkish fire, rifle and guns.

The sight of the men coming from the trenches was too sickening, covered in mud and wet through to the skin, and so they remained all day and night. No waterproofs, no change of clothing, not even socks. Many cases admitted to hospital with Ague fever, pneumonia, bronchitis, dysentery, rheumatism, besides the wounded. Several of the Sepoys died from sheer exposure, and to make matters worse the most depressing news about the 'Relief Force' and notice to say everyone from tomorrow to be on half rations. And still it rains.

I had a most impossible journey to the cemetery with funeral party, the roads being knee deep in mud. Everyone is feeling it a great effort to keep cheerful. Hospital in appalling state—rain all dripping through the roof where great holes have been made by the shells, on to patients' beds and into their cubicles where some poor beggars are lying on the ground, and it is impossible to stop it. No lights at nights as no more oil, candles bought at exorbitant prices etc. Spent whole day in trying to cheer up patients in hospital, not so easy a task as there is nothing cheerful to tell them.

22 January. Roads and whole of town almost impossible to get about in. Saw soldiers who had been in the trenches all last night, they looked blue with cold and

were one mass of wet mud—yet all they said was 'Well, sir, we've got to stick it.' Wonderful chap, Tommy Atkins . . .

24 January . . . Our troops visited abandoned Turkish trenches and found lots of literature exhorting our native troops to kill their English officers, mutiny and come over to the Turks and be under the protection of Allah, telling them they would be far better treated and have more pay. Other pamphlets stated that the Germans and Austrians etc. were going to conquer the whole world. These pamphlets were tied on a stone and thrown from the 1st line trenches to ours and written in Hindustani so that the Indians could read them . . .

27 January . . . Met General Townshend while visiting patients. He said 'Hullo, I haven't seen you for a long while.' My reply was 'You can't expect to, if you will never attend any of my services!' He seemed very cheerful and said we had ample food for 100 more days, and that the troops now coming to help General Aylmer's Relief Force were a healthy number—but he had not said how many in yesterday's communique to the troops for fear of the enemy getting hold of it . . . Tomorrow we have to eat partly horseflesh . . .

30 January . . . Three shells came along, one hit an opening I am always going through, another fell unexploded, which an ass of a native brought to my room on his shoulder! Perhaps he thought it would do to add to my collection . . .

1 February . . . Visited soldiers in their dugouts. They took me round and with pride showed me where all the fighting had taken place, and where the Turks made a rush in hundreds—as many as came were killed. There they lie still, and it is over six weeks ago! Officers and men alike, lying just as they were shot—whole rows of them.

There was one dead Turk so close to the Fort wall you could touch him with your hand. Another twenty yards out had been fed by our men for two days—the third day they did not throw the food quite far enough and they made signs to him to stretch out his rifle and draw it in. To those who did not know what he was doing it must have looked as though he was trying to shoot someone —he was just getting his food in when he was shot by one of our Indian soldiers some way off. There he lay with his jaw all broken—gone quite black—a truly dreadful sight.

Another was shot some way off and he fell close to the parapet of his own trenches—all he could do was to raise one arm and wave it in the air. His comrades in the trench could not see him and so there he lay for three days. His comrades then began to deepen their trench and they threw soil over him—quite innocent of the fact—and still he was raising his arm helplessly.

Another Turk with a bump for the 'comical' was in a trench digging away merrily and every now and then he would flourish his spade-head above the trench as much as to say 'Cheeroh ye British'. One of our fellows got the spade with a bullet and broke it. There was no work for some time, when slowly and in a very tired way up came the spade again with a bandage on its head! . . .

12 February. Unable to write up diary for some days now with another attack of colic . . .

It's really wonderful how this Division has stood the strain all this while i.e. constant watching, constant working and constant waiting—waiting for the Relieving Force which never comes. Little do people at home realise what the soldiers are really going through. They may read account after account of their hardships but they can never realise things properly when in an easy chair, in a safe place and surrounded by comforts.

The state of the soldiers' clothes is pathetic—some practically in rags—boots with great holes in them—no buttons—no shirt. Wood is so scarce for fires that anyone caught with it is to be shot. It is a pitiful sight to see the British Tommies in dozens, ill clad, cold and underfed, straggling up from the trenches into the village to buy a few Arab chapatties to take back to the trenches to stave off their hunger.

17 February. My 36th birthday! Odd to have spent this as well as Christmas in a Siege. Jolly fine day—rain appears to have gone. This is good. Had a tub to celebrate the day and then went down to the Officers' ward to tiffin with Major Thompson etc. We ate one of his Battery horses!—horrible thought—after the splendid way these animals have worked for us. Had it not been for them we should most certainly all have been killed or prisoners. They had actually worked a Birthday cake—made of oatmeal and jolly good . . .

My birthday has been made still more memorable by a message we received from the King Emperor to General Townshend, as follows: 'I together with all your fellow Countrymen continue to follow with admiration the gallant fighting of the Troops under your command against great odds and every possible effort is being made to support your splendid resistance. George R.I.' . . .

23 February. A very interesting day. At 9 a.m. I walked down with my orderly to the first line trenches where General Delamain, about 16 officers and 80 Dorsets were waiting for a Service. It was a broad trench, some 12 feet deep, with platforms and I stood between two traverses. It was a most unique service and possibly the very first time one had been held in any first line of trenches. It was a glorious morning and perfectly still and calm excepting for the boom of guns down the river of our Relieving Force and the occasional crack of a Turkish

sniper's rifle. The Service seemed to impress everyone very considerably and the hymns were sung well and they had a deep and tremendous meaning for all of us.

I then went on to the Dorset Officers' Mess and Celebrated the Holy Communion at which 15 were present. It was a novel experience Celebrating out in the open—the blue of heaven one's church roof—there was very little room for the men to kneel and it was with bare knees upon rough ground that they knelt to receive those Sacred mysteries—and I doubt not that these Services will remain a lifelong memory to each one of us . . .

On the way back I met General Townshend. He stopped me and said 'Well and how are you? Only a few days more, only a very few days more, before we are relieved now.' Then he added 'Why, Job is nowhere now—he is not in the race at all!' . . .

8 March. This morning we had to read the following communique from General Townshend: 'I take the troops of all ranks into my confidence again and repeat the following two telegrams from General Aylmer from which they will see that our Relieving Force has again failed to relieve us . . . In order to hold out I am killing a large number of horses so as to reduce the quantity of grain eaten every day and I have had to reduce your ration. It is necessary to do this in order to keep our flag flying. I am determined to hold out and I know you are with me in this, heart and soul.' . . .

Yesterday evening a Turkish officer came to our lines with a flag of truce. It was from the Turkish Commander asking us to surrender—saying they all admired our pluck in holding out so long—that we had done all that could be expected of us and that, as General Aylmer had again failed to relieve us, there was only one thing for us to do. General Townshend replied that he was much obliged for their advice but that if they didn't mind we would try and hold out a little longer. The Turkish officer presented him with 100 cigarettes, saying he knew we must be short of such things. Odd thing war!

18 March . . . Bomb from German aircraft scored direct hit on General Hospital. 18 killed outright, 30 injured. Awful scenes . . .

27 March . . . I called on the officers of the 67th Punjabis . . . Walked back with Captain Startin, R.A.M.C. Suddenly we heard a cry of pain and saw a Sepoy had been hit. Startin and I ran to him and found he had a bullet through his chest. It was lodged in his shoulder at the back. Poor chap, he was soaked in blood, but Startin fixed him up and organised a stretcher. Shortly afterwards Startin and I were standing wondering which trench to make a bolt for, when a bullet hit the parapet a few inches away. The further we went, the worse it got! . . .

Eventually I just set course for what I hoped was Kut and arrived safely at last and not too late for dinner (such as it is!). I was truly tired, though, and felt once again that Providence had watched over me—many bullets had passed close by. After supper I went round to the hospital to find two more brave soldiers had passed away. Requiescent in pace.

29 March . . . An aircraft flew over (one of ours) and dropped a parcel. Little did I think there would be anything for me, but lo and behold when I returned I found on my table a bundle of letters. I had not heard from England or India for 4 months. It was indeed a breath of fresh air to hear from home again, and everyone seemed quite all right . . .

30 March . . . Many Mohammedans have deserted to the enemy (co-religionists) . . .

31 March . . . For vegetables we get weeds picked out of the grass and made into a kind of spinach. Arab

tobacco is pretty beastly with much palm leaf mixed in it. It's known as the Kut 'sore throat cut' . . .

5 April . . . All this week I have been laying stress on the significant fact that the Collect for this week has this petition, 'that we may mercifully be relieved.' I firmly believe that before this week is out we shall be free men again. This is our earnest prayer . . .

6 April . . . At 5 p.m. I went to take General Townshend's photo. He shewed me a long letter from Lord Curzon. He says 'Keep up heart and be proud that it has been reserved for you to do a big thing for England in the hour of her need.' The General was most cheery . . .

8 April . . . A message came late at night to say 'all going well' with the Relieving Force. A great noise of guns at 6.30 p.m. They must have been covering some attack. I went up to the observation post to watch our guns. It is vastly fascinating. The river is going down but weather looks threatening. Still a lot of thunder about . . .

9 April. At 4 a.m. a terrible bombardment down stream. They must be making a terrific attack. It was just like Fireworks and a magnificent display at that. Well, Gorringe seems to be doing all right. It's a good job for us he is for in 6 days our food will have given out. As I write shells are screaming overhead and bursting in our lines. They are Turkish 40 lb Howitzers. I hope they won't shorten the fuse!

At 11.30 a.m. it was reported that the Turks were massing for a Counter Attack. This is just what our people love them to do, as they are bound to lose heavily—and our guns will thin the ranks somewhat. Artillery duels went on most of the day. It was all quiet at 6.30 p.m. when some 30 gathered for Evensong in the little Chapel. We said special prayers for our Relieving Force and our people at home and sang hymn 595 for

'Absent Friends'. The patients in the General Hospital seemed depressed at 9.30 p.m. when I went round as they had got hold of a rumour that Gorringe had had a reverse and that our rations were again to be decreased.

10 April. The patients were not far wrong as the following communique was issued by General Townshend to the Troops: 'The result of the attack of the Relief Force is that it has not yet won its way through . . . I am compelled therefore to appeal to you all to make a determined effort to eke out our scanty means so that I can hold out for certain till our comrades arrive and I know I shall not make the appeal to you in vain . . . The whole British Empire, let me tell you, is ringing now with our defence of Kut. You will all be proud to say one day, "I was one of the Garrison at Kut", and as for Plevna and Ladysmith we have outlasted them also . . .'

Well, this is terribly disappointing—but it cannot be helped. We still go on believing we shall be freed—but it is hardest of all on the sick and wounded, they are liable to get terribly depressed and it is not to be wondered at. Poor things. They *do* have a rotten time. Nothing will be too good for them when they get out of this . . .

11 April . . . Saw the Prisoners working in the cemetery. Shall soon have it tidy again and more crosses are being put up daily—latterly iron ones have been made as the wooden ones have been stolen, presumably for fire wood—miserable wretches.

At 1 p.m. Captain Cane, R.A.M.C., shewed me a 'dangerously ill' report about General Houghton. I saw him at 3 p.m. suffering from acute enteritis. The doctors were giving him intervenal serum injections. At 5 I saw him again, at 7.15 Cane told me he was dying, when I went and prayed with him and commended him to God's Safe Keeping. At 9.30 he rallied but passed away at 6.30 a.m. next morning. This is a terrible blow to us all.

He was a charming man and a great friend of mine. At 8.30 p.m. there was a terrific storm.

12 April. General Houghton buried at 3.30 p.m. Huge funeral. Over 150 officers and about 100 men. The Norfolks supplied funeral party. General Townshend and Staff and Brigadiers all present. The hailstorm had made the ground so bad that a special roadway had to be made to the cemetery. The 'Last Post' was sounded and the party presented arms. A very impressive Service. In the middle of the Service the Turkish batteries began to shell us heavily. General Houghton's hat and sword were placed on the coffin which was covered by a large Union Jack. The Emblem of all that he had fought and died for. And yet not all, for this is GOD's War. And so the thought comes to one—'Why should anyone be pitied who had died for his Country and his God' . . .

13 April. Rather seedy and bad night rather. It is no wonder when one considers one's food! The marvel is we have kept as well as we have . . .

After supper I could not sit in the horrid little room full of fumes of that Arab tobacco. I could not read in my room for I have no light and so I wandered to the Gunners' observation post. I had not been there long when I saw shells bursting all along the skyline down the river. They were shells of our Relieving Force. I sat in the moonlight very intent—when I saw a red rocket go up—it was a Turkish sign to say the enemy are advancing for an attack. Then rifle fire could be heard in loud bursts and I knew that a battle had begun.

I watched for half an hour and then, as it got colder and I was not feeling very well, I went to bed in the dark, but not before going in to my little Chapel to ask God that our Relieving Force might have a good success . . .

Between now and the surrender 16 days later, Spooner's belief in the power of prayer (a belief to which General Townshend at least paid lip service) must have been tested to the uttermost. From the remaining four entries in his siege diary there is no telling what passed in his mind as those special prayers requested by the General winged their way heavenward from the Garrison to no apparent avail. But from his last compressed entry, covering Easter Week, it is apparent that his own faith remained unshaken.

Monday 17 April–23 (Easter Day). One fears to think what will happen to the Garrison if we are not soon relieved. Everyone is wasting away. Many soldiers are dying from gastro-enteritis—which is really only another name for starvation. It is all too pitiful to think about—no medical comforts or foods now—things are getting beyond endurance.

This week is Holy Week—I am having a Celebration each morning and evening Service at 6.30 p.m. There have been soldiers for every Service. On Thursday I took Lantern Service in the 1st line trenches for the Dorsets when about 85 men attended voluntarily, and on Saturday I took one for the Royal West Kents and Hants Territorials when we had to crouch behind a wall because of the bullets—about 80 of them turned up also voluntarily—in fact I think all who could manage it turned up.

I cannot explain the impressiveness of these Services. All Services now, whether in dugouts, trenches, Fort or Chapel, are all taken to the sound of the guns of our Relieving Force. I do not think hymns have ever been sung or prayers made with greater earnestness.

The diary breaks off here. It resumes on the day of the capitulation, with the Turkish troops pouring into Kut on a rampage of looting (even from British officers in the streets and the hospital's sick and wounded) and the start of a sickening programme of executions, the victims being Arabs and Jews who were judged to have assisted the British in any way.

Each morning one saw the bodies of dead and dying hanging on tripod gallows set up on the river banks. The Turks' method was to hang a man by the neck to the top of the tripod and then ease the legs of the tripod until the man's feet were well off the ground, when the victim was left to be slowly strangled to death.

Spooner was ten days in occupied Kut before being put aboard a paddle-steamer for Baghdad with the Garrison's surviving 220 British and 200 Indian officers. The sick and wounded apart, his chief concern was the fate of the cemetery in which he had so often officiated, with its neatly kept graves and proudly inscribed wooden and iron crosses.

I took the precaution of interviewing the Turkish Commandant and explaining to him our great anxiety about this cemetery. He promised that he would have it respected, and sent his orderly with me to show him the exact spot, and gave his orders that it was not to be molested in any way. The next day, however, I took a funeral there and found that all the wooden crosses had been stolen, and on the following day all the iron ones had gone. Footpaths had been made right across the graves, the wall of the cemetery was broken down and the place resembled an ordinary thoroughfare.

Thereafter it was the fate of the living rather than the dead that was to haunt Spooner—the barely living 2,592 British Tommies, separated from their officers, for whom the real agony had only begun. During the siege 1,746 of the Garrison had been killed or died of disease. In captivity some 1,700 British and 1,300 Indian other ranks were to die—as stragglers from the stumbling columns of parched and starving prisoners herded by the whips and rifle butts of their mounted guards across the desert, as disease-ridden near-corpses in stinking overcrowded prison camps, as slave labourers on railways.

That Spooner and his two fellow padres saw it as their duty to stick by the other rank prisoners is clear from a letter they wrote to the Turkish Minister of War on their arrival at their officers' POW camp in Turkey in July 1916. It reveals that after the capitulation the Turkish Commandant had asked them whether it was their wish to remain with the POWs or to join the sick troops aboard a Red Cross boat for repatriation. 'Our answer was that it was our duty to remain with our soldiers as long as it was possible for us to be with them and minister to them.'

In the early stages of Spooner's captivity, which involved a 600-mile trek over parched and rugged terrain in Turkey, his own experiences were gruelling enough. But he makes light of them in comparison with the horrific glimpses he had of the fate of the other ranks. The first was during the five-day river voyage to Baghdad when a contingent of 780 Tommies and Sepoys, too weak to continue the desert march, were driven towards the paddle-steamer.

> . . . I saw them beaten with sticks and the butt end of rifles, sick, unable to march. It was impossible to take them all on board and we had to leave 250 Indians on the river banks. It made my blood boil to witness the treatment of our troops and to hear their horrible stories. I saw great bruises on their sides and backs—they had been driven and beaten for 3 days, their only food 2 Turkish biscuits each. Some were in a demented state when they arrived on board. Now soldiers are lying almost on top of each other . . .

It was with a party of 30 officers and 20 orderlies that Spooner and his fellow padres found themselves fighting to

keep going on a marathon march spread over six weeks.
Their record was 45 miles in 14 hours, and part of Spooner's
diary entry for that day may serve for the rest:

> . . . Marching on and on our convoy had become much
> extended, with two miles between the first and last, some
> walking a few yards and then sitting down, some crawl-
> ing along with the aid of a stick, some being helped by
> others, the more fortunate riding on a few donkeys. We
> came to hill-top after hill-top, only to see the head of the
> convoy still struggling on . . .

Such hardships paled into insignificance when Spooner
discovered what had happened to numbers of survivors of
the other ranks' death march from Kut. The setting is two
prison camp 'hospitals' in towns passed through en route to
the comfortable quarters that awaited him in an officers'
camp at the end of his road. It was a contrast that was to prey
on his mind for the rest of the war.

29 June. Nisibin . . . I thought I had witnessed horror
enough in these frightful hospital conditions, but another
more terrible sight had got to be seen. There was a small
dark dank room, with no windows to it, only a few feet
square. Something told me to go inside this room, and
there to my horror I saw two British soldiers, absolutely
naked, lying in their own faeces, which had not been
cleaned up for several days.

They were both dying and, thank God, one was
unconscious. The other said to me 'Oh, sir, please kneel
down and ask that God may let me die quickly. I can no
longer stand these horrors.'

On talking to other invalids living quite close I was
told they had tried time after time to be allowed to attend
to these poor fellows, and at least to clean them, but the

guard would not even allow them to enter the room or even give them any water.

Can anyone conceive the terror that must have gone through these men's minds before they died, knowing full well that that was the object for which they had been put there? What could one do but to kneel down and say a prayer and commend them to God's keeping?

I was able to leave a little money behind, and made arrangements that these poor fellows should have some milk brought to them, but whether this was carried out or not I cannot say. Later I met some soldiers who had survived this terrible treatment and learned that that was the Turkish method. They waited till they thought someone was going to die and then they placed him in this room of terror and merely left . . .

5 July. Islahie . . . I went to see the German Commandant in the town and urged him to visit the camp. At first he refused to believe we were British officers when he saw the state we were in. We then brought him to visit our sick in those dreadful tents. He had sent for his own German doctor and together they went in to one of the sick tents. He soon came out, however, saying 'I am sorry, I simply cannot see such things as these.' It may be remarked that the suffering must have been pretty bad for a German to have made such a statement . . .

From his camp at Kastamoni, Spooner later sent a letter to the Secretary of State for War in London detailing atrocities that had come to his notice (after the war Spooner's records were among the mass of evidence sifted by a Committee of Enquiry into Breaches of the Laws of War, which led to the trial of the worst offenders).

At Nisibin, Spooner wrote, 'the dead are buried naked in two feet of earth, like cats or dogs. Immediately they are dead their boots and clothes are at once stolen by the Turkish orderlies. So anxious are they for them to die that the stretcher is brought and put alongside them long before they are dead and in full view of them.'

Prisoners were flogged and bastinadoed for trifling off-ences. 'It is impossible in many places to be free of lice and yet if a British soldier is found with a louse he is not only unmercifully flogged but compelled to eat the louse.' In labour gangs prisoners were compelled to work 11 hours a day on small portions of boiled barley and mouldy bread —'they are dying at the rate of 4 and 5 a day in many camps.'

In a letter to the Turkish authorities, asking them to allow him to visit various other rank camps, Spooner wrote: 'It seems a terrible thing to think that so many of our troops, undergoing such dreadful suffering, have no Chaplain to visit them in hospital, to be with them when they are dying, or to bury them when they are dead. I know how intensely the soldiers feel this, and how they would appreciate the presence of a Chaplain amongst them to take Services regularly in their camps.'

His appeal was in vain. For the last 2½ years of the war his ministrations were largely confined to officers and orderlies. But one unexpected outlet for his Christianly concern he did find. The Greek community in Kastamoni, like others under Turkish rule, was cruelly oppressed and in a state of destitution. Surreptitiously Spooner organised among his fellow POWs gifts of food and money, which drew from the head priest of the community two letters of thanks and the presentation of a silver ikon, which was to be among his most prized possessions in later life.

Father Anastasias's flowery letters, beginning 'Very dear brother in Jesus Christ' and ending 'Asking you to accept my kiss in Jesus Christ, I remain your very devoted Brother', must have seemed a bit overwhelming to an Anglican not prone to effusions. The second letter reveals that Spooner's final concern as a captive padre (as it had been after the occupation of Kut) was that the graves of the British dead in the camp cemetery should not be neglected or defiled.

. . . You have made me a request, dear Brother in Jesus Christ, the fulfilment of which I believe to be my duty, not only as a priest, not only as a Greek, but as a man. You mention the tombs of your comrades who have died in exile for the glory of their country. These tombs are equally dear to us the Greeks and when you are gone we will concentrate our gratitude on them. In these tombs we see gleaming the fire of divine enthusiasm, we see the valour of your comrades and the imperishable qualities of your great nation, Holy Albion, the supreme protector of right, the mother of Liberty. Leave these tombs in my hands as a priest, leave them in the hearts of the Greeks of Kastamoni, who bless you . . .

Spooner's diary entry beneath this letter is brief: 'We feel now that the Greek priest Anastasias will do his utmost to look after the Cemetery when we have gone.' But it is in the nature of a tailpiece to all that he had striven for. Denied access to those of the living he felt most needed his help, he had at least kept faith with the dead.

For Spooner the armistice brought release from captivity but not from the intolerable strains that had built up over the past three traumatic years. It was later clear that he was returned to duty far too quickly, after only 8 months' 'sick leave' in England, part of it spent in assisting the War Office and India Office in drawing up a dossier on all the officers and men who had lost their lives or gone missing.

Back in India he met and married the daughter of Major General George Harris, Commander of the India Medical Service in Bengal. Two sons were born. But that horrific past was catching up with him.

The progress of Spooner's tragic deterioration is revealed in a 1927 report by Lt.-Col. S. Haughton, a 6th Division medical officer who had known him during the siege and its aftermath, and who continued to be his medical attendant in India. Of the early years he writes:

> The starvation and strain of the 5 months' siege, followed by a 500 miles march through the deserts of Turkey, the hardships, monotony and at times uncertainty of life which all prisoners were subject to, left its undoubted and indelible mark on many of my brother officers and men, as characterised by definite neurasthenic symptoms and abnormal psychoses. To my certain knowledge several of my brother officers have never regained what one would describe as a normal balanced brain, and several are in mental hospitals.

In India Haughton found that Spooner's physical health had been further undermined by 'very serious maltreatment on the part of a Turkish dentist, sepsis setting in on the upper jaw after several teeth had been extracted or partly extracted.' By 1923 he was of the opinion that Spooner was unfitted for work on account of insomnia, depression and irritability ('the slightest upset in the daily round of life made him lose his temper—I have witnessed these absurd explosions in his own house').

But Spooner declined to face the fact that he was a sick man, even though he could have accompanied his wife when she was invalided home after a serious illness. In 1924 he was sent as Chaplain to a particularly large and outlandish district. Two years later he had a serious nervous breakdown and was invalided home for good.

The 16 years Spooner spent in a Nottingham nursing home specialising in mental casualties of the war remained a total blank in his memory after his recovery. Because he was unable to recognise his wife Maud when she visited him, she only once took their eldest son to see him, a distressing occasion not to be repeated. Pat Spooner recalls:

He was virtually out of this world, in a limbo. Though he was able to get up and move about, he was in a Rip van Winkle existence, a mental blackout, reading nothing, not interested in anything or anybody at all. When my mother was finally asked if she would give her permission for him to undergo electric shock treatment, then in an experimental stage, she agreed to it as a last resort. Thank God she did, for it cured him. It cured him completely—a real miracle cure.

The last 22 years of Spooner's life, up to his death in 1964 aged 84, seemed like a compensation for all that had gone before. Says Pat Spooner:

For me it was not until later in life that I really got to know my father and to discover what a marvellous man he was. After serving in the Second World War I worked for many years in America and I returned to find him happily in harness again as a curate in the Lake District, where his family had roots.

After all those years in a state of suspended animation, he was making up for lost time. It was as though he had been reborn. He would be up at dawn, going for long country walks or fishing (his great passion). He had a bit of a wild streak, prone to tearing about the countryside on his motor-bike, with cassock flying in the wind, much to the terror of the local populace. But they all loved him. Perhaps with memories of Kut, he was particularly assiduous as a hospital visitor. His faith remained unshaken. I have pages and pages of the sermons he took so much care over and that must have gone to the hearts of his congregations.

Holiday snapshots taken of Spooner with his eldest son and his grandson, sailing on Lake Windermere, basking in a sun-drenched garden, show a slight venerable figure, with bushy white eyebrows and a lined, but benign face. In old age he was able to look back with equanimity on his Kut experiences. At the annual reunions of the Kut Association (now disbanded for lack of membership) he conducted the service beside the Kut plaque in the crypt of St Paul's Cathedral. Shortly before his death he was taking a great interest in the forthcoming BBC television series on the Great War, travelling to London to discuss the Kut episode with the producer and showing the photographs he had taken during the siege. He was even, with the help of a nephew in Kendal, starting to make a book out of his diaries.

What most intrigued Spooner when he finally got to know his eldest son, was to discover affinities in their war experiences. Pat Spooner had also been a prisoner-of-war, captured during the desert war, and had also been awarded the MBE (for escaping from an Italian POW camp). More remarkably he had earlier gone from Sandhurst to join a Gurkha regiment in India, in 1941 had served with an expeditionary force of the Indian Army in Iraq (formerly Mesopotamia), and had taken the opportunity of paying a brief visit to Kut.

I knew very little at that time about my father's experiences during the siege [says Spooner]. Had I read his diary I would have made a much closer inspection. As it was I could only tell him that I found Kut a hell-hole of a place, a drab stinking little town, which (when I was there) must have been the hottest spot on earth. Of course he asked if there was anything to show that once a besieged British garrison had held out there for five months. All I had seen had been the crumbling remains of some trenches around the town. No indication of where the hospital had been. No sign of a cemetery.

In the Christmas week of 1964, just 49 years after he had begun his ministrations as a padre in the chapel, hospital and trenches of beleagured Kut, Spooner was laid to rest in a country churchyard in his beloved Lakeland. In a letter to Pat Spooner, Mrs Helen Elliott, wife of the Rector at Windermere, wrote:

Your father will be sadly mourned by all his numerous friends, who stretched literally from one end of England to the other, for he had a gift of making—and keeping —friends. He will be greatly missed in the Church, too, for he has played an amazingly active part in the ministry right up to the last. He was a most ardent and vigorous hospital chaplain, where his ready sympathy and understanding for those who were confined to bed were well appreciated.

He greeted every day with a joyfulness that is not often seen—much less in one of his age—and regarded each day as a bonus from God and lived it to the full. No time for an extra 'lie in' for him—he regarded bed as rather a waste of time and was always up early and to bed late. He even wrote his Christmas cards the day before he died . . .

Few padres can have weathered such ordeals as Spooner was subjected to. One is reminded of General Townshend's comment to him at the height of the siege: 'Why, Job is nowhere now—he is not in the race at all!' As with Job, he had tribulations heaped upon him. As with Job, his faith stood firm. In the darkest hour he never capitulated. And patience was rewarded.

CHAPTER TWO

ONWARD CHRISTIAN SOLDIERS

EQUATING CHRISTIANITY WITH war came naturally to the Rev David Railton, an Anglican padre on the Western Front who was to achieve fame as the instigator of the tomb of the Unknown Warrior in Westminster Abbey. His father, George Scott Railton, had been William Booth's 'first lieutenant' at the founding of the Salvation Army and had been largely responsible for the military metaphors and 'war songs' used in promoting its militant evangelism.

For George Railton, who spent much of his life on missions abroad, all the world was a battlefield and race and creed were of no account in the saving of souls. For him 'the German War' was a phrase used to describe the four years he spent, from 1886 to 1890, organising an 'underground Army' in Germany, often in the face of virulent hostility. On a mission to South Africa during the Boer War he showed as much concern for the Boers and the native Africans as for the British.

It was in a spirit far removed from this that David Railton conducted his ministrations to the Tommies during his three years at the front. For him the rousing 'war songs' he had known from childhood, and which by now had been heard in cities around the world, had a strictly limited application. Onward Christian Soldiers referred exclusively to the Allies,

particularly the Tommies. In the Salvationist hymn com-
posed by his father (to the tune of 'Men of Harlech'),
beginning 'Christian, rouse thee! War is raging/God and
fiends are battle waging', there could now be no doubt as to
who were the fiends: the Boche.

In letters home to his wife Railton almost invariably refers
to the Germans as 'the Boche' or 'the Prussians'. At one stage
during the Battle of the Somme (when he was awarded the
Military Cross) he describes them as 'unsporting, low
brutes'. He even seems to have assumed that God would be
turning a deaf ear to the pleas of Christians in the enemy
camp. 'We hear that the Archbishop of Cologne is going to
pray for the Boche on a certain day shortly', he writes in
one letter. 'Never before have I understood the meaning
of that prayer in the Psalms, "Let his prayer be turned to
sin."'

To Railton the 'cross of Jesus going on before' was
synonymous with the Union Jack. In one letter, referring to
the effect he has discovered when the Union Jack is hung
lengthwise, he writes: 'I never realised before what a
wonderful cross of sacrifice that deep red is. I am very keen
that men everywhere should learn that our National Flag is
the symbol of Christ and not a mere series of crosses used for
commercial and secular purposes.'

George Railton had died in 1913 at the age of 64, mourned
by Salvationists around the world, and there is no knowing
what his reactions would have been to the challenging spiritual issues raised by the First World War. It had been a bitter
disappointment to him that his sons David and Nathaniel
(who also served as a chaplain on the Western Front) had not
followed in his steps and donned the international uniform of
the Salvation Army. To them it had been a disruptive
influence, keeping their father away from home for long
periods and making him a virtual stranger to them. Their
mother, though she had been a 'tambourine girl' in the

Salvation Army when they met and was devoted to him, brought them up as Anglicans. It was because she had private means that they were able to study at Keble College, Oxford, and to become ordained into the Church of England.

Though in conflict with his anti-establishment, anti-institutional and ascetically unworldly father (he even forbade his sons to take part in school games), David Railton had the greatest admiration and affection for him. And there were many similarities. Both were engaging personalities, good mixers, with no trace of class snobbery. David's first curacy had been in the slums of Liverpool, where he had met his wife, who worked among the poor for a religious organisation. She came from a well-to-do family (her father owned a chain of grocery shops) and, like his father, he never had to contend with financial problems.

On the surface Railton's letters to his wife (which she later edited and which regrettably cover only the first 15 months of his three years' service at the front) might seem fairly typical of the 'good sport' type of Anglican padre. Knowing his unusual background, they take on a deeper significance. There is an underlying dissatisfaction with the ways of the established church, as being too remote from the ordinary man, and a shift towards ecumenism that was rare at the time. 'I think a new era of religion is coming and I hope so', he writes in one letter. 'The old is very oppressive, whether in Salvation Army barracks, a Congregational Chapel, or the Roman Catholic Church. What is wanted?'

Though there are no direct references to his father, one can sense that Railton constantly had before him his redoubtable example of fearlessness and self-sacrifice. 'His kind of religion', he had written, 'is a thing you have to be frightfully hardy for. You cannot be soft; you have to be a man for his job.' As one of the earlier padres to share the hazards of the Tommy in the trenches, Railton's manliness is not in doubt. The question remains how far the cheery, 'good sport' approach he thought essential had any deep impact in the prevailing atmosphere of fatalism.

That Railton gained at least as much inspiration from the Tommies as they from him seems clear. 'How strange it is that this Army of ours unconsciously carries out our Lord's ideals beyond anything we have seen in churchmen and politicians', he writes. 'I am always telling my lads—You are living the Christ life—why not add to your conduct faith and joy in Him.'

One cannot imagine that George Railton, in his evangelist's role of calling sinners to repentance, would have been content with that, even though he had never experienced the hell on earth that war had become. And one is reminded of a reference in C. E. Montague's war book *Disenchantment* (in a chapter entitled 'The sheep that were not fed') to the 'moments of religious awareness' experienced by many soldiers who had no time for organised religion, but of which the average padre seemed unaware.

'As soon as his genial bulk hove into sight and his cheery rumbustious chaff began blowing about, the shy and uncouth muse of our savage theology flew away', he wrote. 'Once more the talk was all footer and rations and scragging the Kaiser, and how the "Hun" would walk a bit lame after the last knock he had got.'

There are elements of such a padre in Railton's letters, as in his determination to be 'always—at least outwardly—Bright'. But the differences are apparent—a humility that leads him to describe himself as 'only a student trying to learn how the modern Englishman can be drawn to our Lord', a closer identification with the Tommies he served than with the officers in his mess and an absence of that patronising air apparent in some padres' accounts.

The final impression is of a man dedicated to the service of others whose own faith was severely tested in the crucible of war. In a letter written during the bitter winter of 1916–17, with 'death and suffering all around', he writes: 'If our Lord had not suffered on this earth on the cross, I would blaspheme God all day if I believed in God at all. I only believe in God in this war because I believe in Jesus Christ Crucified.' All differences aside, it had been the faith that had sustained his father.

Railton was 32 when he sailed for France, on 11 January 1916, with the 18th Battalion of the Northumberland Fusiliers. His home was at Folkestone, where he had taken up a curacy in 1908 after two years in the Liverpool slum parish where he had met his wife. A daughter was born in 1913 (there were to be three more daughters and one son).

Leading up to the Battle of the Somme, in which he came closest to the horrors of trench warfare, representative extracts from Railton's letters show his rapid acclimatisation to the life of a padre. He rarely indicates where he is writing from, and dates have been omitted from these early extracts as being of slight significance.

We had hours in the train but in a first class carriage. The men were in trucks. Poor boys. Still they were magnificent. This place is called [censored] and is inhabited by 2,500 people.

Don't laugh, but my French with the help of the 3d. phrase book has been of great use to me and of some to my Company Officer, Major Fabrum. 'Padre forward —Come on Padre! For goodness sake tell this man what we want.' 'Right, Sir, I will try.' I take the French people aside to avoid necessary gesticulations being seen and return with the news and the arrangements made. That book has been a boon. I can pronounce the stuff pretty well but my vocabulary is about as much in quantity as is required for a Quaker meeting . . .

I am wonderfully well—my great trouble is the drinking. [Railton's wife was a teetotaller.] The wine is funny stuff, and anyhow I don't wish to take it. The water is filth. The coffee is splendid but one cannot drink it all day. Still I shall find a remedy soon . . .

. . . Last night I went up into a barn to see how the men were tucked in. They all wished me such a hearty goodnight from their straw beds. I am just going to speak a cheery word on the sly (they are in disgrace—not supposed to be spoken to) to two prisoners of our battalion. Both are sentenced to 14 days for drunkenness. Both are chained outside Headquarters to the wheels of gun-carriages. I shall have to pass by and say, 'Cheer up, old sons, come and see me directly you are out of this.' They look fearfully cold. The worst prison at home is a palace by it . . .

. . . I have had my first parade. It was in a factory yard and all went well. For once in a way I pitched the hymns just right, and the men sang well. My heart just aches for them. I spoke on 'Jesus went before them.' . . .

Yesterday we marched to be reviewed by Sir Douglas Haig, Commander-in-Chief, and General Joffre. It was a fine day but the roads were still inches deep in mud. There is an advantage in this, your feet get less blistered. In all we marched about 10 or 12 miles.

As usual we were there—the whole Division—long before the time of the review. We were lined up along the road. The wind got up and the rain came down with it. Officers had no rain coats. The men had their waterproof sheets strapped to their packs. Soon after the rain had stopped, the order came 'Put on cloaks!' The men just had time to get them out and put them on when the order came to fold them up again. They all laughed, and folded them up as best they could with frozen fingers and with the rifles with fixed bayonets in the way all the time.

By and by Sir Douglas Haig and his staff and the

French officers arrived and went slowly by—in Motors! None of them were mounted. The cars were closed. We could only get a second's glimpse of the Chief. Indeed most of us have been disputing ever since as to which car he was in. Still, we each felt we had given a personal salute to our noble Chief and we had been reviewed by him and all sorts of other people in closed up motor cars. The pipes started and away we went back to Somewhere else in France . . .

We were given gas instruction today about 12 miles from here. We all went in London omnibuses. They are painted grey. After a lecture we were given 'Gas' helmets and marched into a room, the door was closed and the gas turned on from a cylinder. This experience gave everyone much confidence as the helmets are quite gas proof. I hated my helmet at first, and thought I should never breathe, and the chemicals are awful—all the brass buttons etc. went green—but I got used to it and feel as fit as ever. What a vile invention these Germans have brought into the world, but what a brilliant antidote our men have made! . . .

News came that there was a raid on the Kent coast on Sunday—May God rid the world of Prussia. I can understand the Psalmist in his fiercest moments. No uncivilised people were worse than the Prussians. It is 10 a.m. I have just read the morning psalms. 'The earth, O Lord, is full of thy mercy,' seems untrue, because man is full of the Devil's cruelty—still—I look at the little birds and hear them sing on this frosty day—and I know there is mercy with God. The guns in the distance in their perpetual roar are nothing, simply nothing to me compared to this—Raid in Kent . . .

This place is a regular target as a rule. Yesterday I was sent to take my first burial. It was of a brave lad called Travis of Windsor Avenue, Gateshead. He was the first to fall of the 18th Northumberland Fusiliers. Well, I had to go on a bike, I was sent the wrong way and part of the way the Germans shelled the district. I got to the trench ¾ of an hour late—but safely—thank God.

We buried the brave lad's remains just behind the trench. Whilst they were preparing I collected a few little blue flowers. A major came and sent off all the men except four as he said it would 'draw fire'. We had the burial service shortened. The men joined in the Lord's Prayer very impressively. No Last Post! I just dropped the flowers on to him and went back along the trench. I had tea with the officers, spoke to the pals of Travis and came away . . .

Two of our men were killed this morning. Both were married. One an R.C. and one a churchman. Walker was married and had six children. He and Reade were both sniped as they had their heads above the parapet. I am going to write to their wives and relations. I spoke with Reade's brother. This is one advantage of being able to go right into the front trenches. You can encourage many a 'broken' lad. Some of them were just crying this morning, and yet when you say, 'Keep up your heart, old lad,' they pull themselves together and say, 'Oh you may be sure of that, Sir.' It is all one long pathos to me . . .

We were going to the trenches yesterday. After a while we came to a farm. It had been heavily shelled. At the entrance there was a great door and on the door a notice to citizens as to what they are to do in the event of a gas attack. A strongly built maiden stood reading this notice. Her hands were clasped firmly behind her. She was a girl of about 18 to 20. As we came nearer we could see that she had a strong and indeed beautiful face.

Captain Swinburn agreed with me that it was a study of a brave woman. He exclaimed, 'Fancy her being here at all.' She turned quietly, and as we passed she gave us a strong look as much as to say, 'I don't care what comes now—I'm not afraid of their cursed Gas or anything else.' God bless and protect that girl. Oh the unflinching pluck of that daughter of France! Jean d'Arc would bless her and indeed our Lord Himself would surely give her His own strong Benediction. I wish I were as plucky and resolute . . .

Today brought me a most joyful experience. All the chaplains of this division met the Senior Chaplain, the Revd. Harry Blackburne. I can hardly tell you what a help he was to me. He began by telling us that Sir Douglas Haig had said before a meeting of Generals that he was one of the men who believed in prayer. Then he proceeded to give us the straightest imaginable talk I have ever heard given to any clergy since the days when the little Bishop of Liverpool (Bishop Chavasse) used to make us all feel humbled and long to improve.

Blackburne went on to say that a General had imitated three parsonic voices, that were no use in the army. Then he went deeply into spiritual matters. He has been out here since the beginning of the war. He gave us his experiences as to how to use opportunities. He simply opened my eyes and filled my heart with enthusiasm. He urged us to make 'reverent experiments', not just for the sake of the army but for the future of England. He told us to celebrate at any time. Day and night—in the trenches or out. He had never been used to anything but early celebrations himself—he always tells the men so, but he thought our Lord would be pleased with us if we held His service at any time just now under such conditions. At the end he spoke so kindly to me and I came away full of a deep joy which I cannot explain on paper . . .

I went into the R.C. Church here tonight. I knelt at the altar rail. All was still for a while. Presently an English R.C. chaplain came and knelt in the centre of the Altar rail and began 'Benediction'. The church was all in darkness. He couldn't see who I was.

I took some chocolate to a sentry just now, and last night a jam sandwich and also bread and cheese to another one. Naughty of me to do such a thing in the army! but it is not wicked, and I saw no red-tape as it was very dark. After his fierce northern challenge the sentry took his surprise gift with glee—I left him munching it—with the caution that he was not to take too big mouthfuls at a time or else he would be unable to challenge people! I asked him if he knew the Church's order for all sentries. When I told him it was 'Watch and Pray', he said 'Yes, Sir', and I left him contentedly surprised also.

. . . Bennett, the R.C., was buried by one of our chaplains in mistake—but I don't suppose the Great Redeemer cares which chaplain buries a man as long as it is done reverently, after the kindly manner of Joseph of Arimathea. Do not you think so? . . .

I have only time to tell you of a wonderful experience I had today. I was out of the trenches for a few hours, but went back at night (first line—fire line). At about 11.45 p.m. I was in one bay with a group of men. The sentry was on the fire-step and I sat and talked with the others. We talked of everything and as 12 midnight approached I spoke of Ireland, the Tyneside Irish and St. Patrick's day.

On the stroke of 12 I stood up and said to the 12 men who were free in the bay, 'It's just after 12—just St. Patrick's Day, shake hands all round, lads.' They stood up and each man gave me a very hearty grip. 'Now' I said 'we will say the Lord's Prayer together if no one has any objection.' They joined me heartily with heads un-covered. I then gave them the Blessing with raised hand and they said 'Amen.' We had scarcely sat down when one of them said—'Beg pardon, Sir, but the day is my birthday.' I gave him ¾ packet of Baccy which had been given to me. Then I sat down and told them I had some shamrock sent. I opened my box and gave each man a sprig and put one in my own cap round the cross. After a while I left them and went on to all the bays of the Companies.

In April Railton was transferred to the 47th London (Territorial) Division stationed near Vimy Ridge, one of the most fiercely contested sectors on the front. Overlooking the now-ruined coal mining town of Lens, the ridge had become a warren of tunnels at many levels, from which mines were exploded by both sides. It was in this macabre and menacing setting that Railton celebrated Easter.

24 April. On Good Friday there was so much work in hand supplying working parties in the trenches and in carrying out lots of other work that no services were practical before 12 noon and that would conflict with the mid-day meal. So we gave out a 2.30 p.m. service in a place in the village which is to be a cinema in the far off days to come. It is now a damp barn-like building made airy at the sides by Bosche shells but there is a roof and a floor with no puddles.

At 2.30 p.m. 4 men arrived. We began at 2.37 to sing 'When I survey the wondrous Cross'. Gradually our numbers increased until there were 12 of us. As I read part of the story of the Passion the loud voice of a sergeant could be heard drilling a squad, and the thud of a football also. We sang 'There is a green hill' and 'Rock of Ages'. I spoke on the two remarks of the centurion at the Cross —'Truly this man was the Son of God' and 'Certainly this was a righteous man', and did my best to encourage them. I told them that there were fewer men even than our number at Calvary—on the side of Jesus Christ—yet the once hesitant disciples plucked up courage afterwards and lived and worked and died for Jesus and built up His Church by His grace.

Later I was on my way to [censored] as a wire had come earlier in the day to say I would need a digging party. I got there soon after 8.30 p.m. The party did not arrive from the fire trench till after 10 p.m. We made our way in the darkness—you may not even use a flashlight as the ground is under observation from the Boche. I had only one N.C.O. and 3 men but they dug away until about 11 p.m. We then went to the trench mortuary with the rain still streaming down.

We carried our brave hero's mortal remains with the greatest of difficulty over the rough ground and a narrow plank bridge and buried him as reverently as we can here. Indeed, it is wonderful to me—to stand there with a group of soldiers at such a time. The picks and shovels are put aside. We all stand quietly by and I lead the service. The Verey lights go up now and again lighting up our faces and guns keep up their usual squabbling with each other; and then all these men say the Lord's Prayer so firmly and evenly loudly, so that you feel they really mean it. And then they fill in the grave and go back to the fire line.

26 April. The Brigade moves today, another one takes our place in the trenches. It is my duty to remain here, and go up to the cemetery tonight in case there are any casualties for me. I have been taking it easy today as I only returned from the cemetery at 4.10 a.m. My little working party were exhausted and we went over the ground rather slowly, and twice we had to fall flat because of machine gun fire. Just as we passed through a ruined village we heard a furious bang. A mine had been exploded, and at once a violent bombardment began, such as I have never heard or seen. It was 3.30 a.m.

We were out of the danger zone. The ground on which we stood was fairly high up, and we could see the lines of the trenches illuminated by the flash of the guns and the flare of the Verey lights. One of my party said, 'It is an attack.' All of us noticed how beautifully the birds were singing. They kept it up during the whole of the bombardment.

When I got up this morning we were given full news. It was an attack and the Boche got into our trenches. Oh! how terrible it makes one feel when England (at home) could prevent it all. Coming home today I saw a bi-plane in a field. It came down because the observer, a young Canadian, was killed—shot through the head by a bullet. Oh, it is all such a mixture of the noblest deeds, of humour and pathos, farce and tragedy, life and death, that this world can ever produce.

28 April. I got back at 5 a.m. this morning from the trenches. At 7 p.m. yesterday they exploded a mine in the lines of one of our battalions. A furious bombardment followed. I stayed until our wounded came along our trench, far behind the actual fire line, and I helped the men who were not stretcher cases. One poor chap had to be piggy-backed down the trench, and he was so heavy. We took it in turns. One of our poor officers was buried alive and several men. Still our men beat the Boche, as they could not get the crater.

29 April. Two of our padres are leaving. One need not go at all. He is simply going because his year is up. It is simply scandalous that all officers here have to stick it for the duration of the war—and then a chaplain who has got to know the men well goes off as he has had enough of it—and as his year is up . . .

That Railton, whose real testing time was yet to come, was increasingly concerned about the fighting men's reactions to padres, and about the future of the church generally, is indicated by a letter written during a rest period after Vimy.

It is strange how the words 'High', 'Low', 'Broad', 'Catholic', disappear out here. I was at a meeting of very experienced Chaplains the other day, and I heard Blackburne say that the words were never used, you never hear them on the lips of officers or men. When we come home we shall have to apply the knowledge we have gained here in our work at home. Things will change. At present I am only a student trying to learn how the modern Englishman can be drawn to our Lord and to His Church in such a way that he will enjoy the experience.

I have not learnt how it can be done yet. So far I have only learnt that our Englishman do not care a pin whether a man is High or Low, Broad or Catholic, or a Dissenter, whether he gives allegiance to Canterbury, Rome or to General Booth. He just cares to see if a man is genuine, and he will come to a service if it appeals to him and is manly, and not simpering or loud. The biretta or the Salvation Army hat amuse equally! He does not mind if a man wears vestments or a surplice so long as he is a man.

What he does need and want in the way of services is difficult to say, I don't know. I only know that generally speaking Folkestone Parish Church Choral Eucharist would be too High for him and the Baptist Chapel too dull. I think a new era of religion is coming and I hope so. The old is very oppressive, whether in Salvation Army barracks, a Congregational Chapel, or the Roman Catholic Church. What is wanted?

On 1 July the Battle of the Somme was launched, that holocaust in which any belief that God was on either side, or even that there was a God at all, must have been hard to sustain. Confidently expected to bring victory to the Allies, it had achieved next to nothing by the time it foundered to an end four months later. There had been over 400,000 British casualties. The 'flower of English manhood' had perished.

It was not until September that the 1/19th Battalion of the City of London Regiment, to which Railton was now attached, went into action, after an intensive period of training. Railton's letters, starting with the gruelling marches from the rear area towards the front, show him in buoyant form, seemingly eager to be where the action was, to be 'there'.

We are all done today, we have had some terrific marches. Yesterday (Sunday) we started at 6.30 a.m. and got in at 8 p.m. It was a roaring hot day. Orders were that no one was to fall out unless unconscious. If he did he would be treated as a deserter. In spite of that 15 fell out of this battalion alone and many more out of other battalions. Out of our 15, ten were unconscious, and the rest had feet so broken and bleeding that no more was possible. One brave laddie actually held out to the end, and then collapsed and was found to have no skin on his feet at all. They were just raw.

Of course many of the men are new. Gradually training will tell. Trench warfare is no use for marching training. I am very well. Thank God I have just enough strength so far. There is no fighting at present, but we are marching 'there'. It was only that I was so tired that I could scarcely crack a joke and yet I am glad to say I sang the songs as lustily as anybody on the last stretch of the march yesterday.

We have just completed another fairly long march. The men are getting fitter. We took a slower, longer step today and only 5 men dropped out. Of course the heat is fearful and so the men get very done. One of them said today on the march, 'I feel exactly like a hard-boiled egg.' We are sleeping tonight in the open, in a lovely orchard.

Of course there is no fighting near us but, as I said, we are on our way 'there' . . .

We left here at 6 a.m. I went on with the billeting officer this time, I generally march with the men. I helped to get billets. Most of the villagers were still abed at 7.15 a.m. Gradually they woke up and in some places came out to see the soldiers, dressing themselves as they came. They were eager to know when the battalions would arrive. In one case a certain madamoiselle retired at once when I told her they would be here in an hour and dressed up in her best clothes including a beautiful French silk apron which they wear on special occasions. She looked a new creature in her blue blouse etc. etc., and doubtless thought she would look her best in the eyes of the British soldier. She must have been disappointed because when our men arrived and were given the halt they just dropped down, sat down and laid down in the road and hardly regarded anybody. They were so hot and tired. But at the same time I do not blame the damsel for rigging out in honour of old England even if it may be meant to draw a little attention to herself . . .

. . . I gave a young Scots officer a piece of that lovely heather, and I said 'I can't do very much for you in your military work but here is a breath from Scotland and I wish you good luck.' He thanked me for it and his eyes seemed a bit full as he popped it away in his pocket book and said, 'That's going over the top with me.' God bless him and all the boys when we get 'there' . . .

. . . I admire our Colonel. Last night as the storm came he gave up his tent for the men. The result is that all the officers are crowded as some of their tents were given up and we all mess under an awning. The men love him for it.

Why are people so less sacrificing in peacetime? If a Colonel—a gentleman—can give up his tent in a storm for the soldiers, why can't a gentleman of like position give up many luxuries for some injured workman? I hope such great things from this war. I can almost see a new England. Of course it will only be in the exact proportion in which we follow our Lord . . .

. . . All the little twinkling candles are out in this bivouac field. Suddenly from across the country road I hear the voice of a sergeant, 'Jock, Jock!' Presently someone answers and the sergeant proceeds, 'You are to parade at Battalion Headquarters at 8 a.m.—fighting order.' The voice sang out so clearly from across the other field.

This is always so here—fighting order—fighting order—fighting order—Each man and each Brigade, Division, Corps and Army—always being called out to stand ready for the day when the real fight comes. I wish we could get more of this spirit into the Church. I love that clear call. Yet—our Lord calls us just as clearly and we refuse or hesitate and so delay His greater Call, and we wonder why the Church is so devilish slow!

For Railton the 'day when the real fight comes' was near.

12 September. We have got 'there'. Our men are waiting their turn. God help us all. We had some splendid services yesterday, I hope they did good. The men are in great form. A good few are inwardly anxious but they put a cheery face on it all. Sometimes this is from a highly religious motive, at other times it is a kind of fatalism. 'What has to be, will be,' they often say.

I myself am at present writing in a dug-out which was in German hands a short while ago. Many guns are just behind us. The vibration is so great that spoons jump in the sugar case or tea cups. It is great fun to watch a man shave. He shaves while another man watches the gun. On the command 'Stop' he stops till the bang has gone, when he resumes shaving!

We had some wonderful services on Sunday. To see 50 or 60 men in a dark building, lighted only by a few candles and one acetylene lamp is wonderful! Your cross is on the wall, and 2 candles and the oak cross on the Altar, the Union Jack underneath. The singing very enthusiastic. Oh! what could I not say as I stand— writing with my gas helmet wrapped on my chest at 'the ready'—about this enemy of God and man!

On 15 September the British launched their third all-out attempt to break through the German defences, and for six weeks Railton was in and out of the fluctuating line. The ten, mostly brief, letters he wrote during the period are probably deliberately understated to avoid causing undue anxiety and distress to his wife. And it is clear that his first experience of 'there' had been a traumatic one. His chief duty appears to have been the clearing of the battlefield and the burial of the remains of officers and men (including his admired Colonel and the Scottish officer to whom he had given that 'lucky' sprig of heather).

Initial objective for the 47th (London) Division, of which Railton's battalion was part, was High Wood, one of the key strongholds of the Somme front, a labyrinth of trenches and concrete dugouts and splintered trees that saw some of the bloodiest hand-to-hand fighting of the war. On 14 July British cavalry had penetrated the wood but been repulsed. On 3 September a ferocious attack by the Cameron High-landers and Black Watch had also been repulsed. Railton's first letter is written five days after the London battalions had finally cleared the wood.

20 September. The battle is over for our men for at least a week. The Brigade has lost over 900, but the positions were won. The Battalion I am with lost 10 officers out of

14 (killed). We are now burying the bonny comrades who were with us before, it is dreadful!

Many men who have stood it all, cannot stand this clearing of the battlefield. I don't know what to tell you, I expect it would be censored. I am writing standing. We are in the open and there is not even a seat after this day's downpour. All goes well with me. I have been wonderfully protected.

Yesterday, after we had done burying, the men were speaking of the shells that were sent over. One of them said, 'You had a very close shave, Sir.' I said, 'Yes, I suppose I did.' Only then did I remember the fact as the private described it that there was a crump and a piece flew just an inch or two past my leg into the earth. As a matter of fact we were all lucky because none actually burst over us. I thanked God, as I do, for sparing me. Only then did I remember all His mercies. The guns roar. Another attack is on but our men are not in this time.

24 September. All goes well with me, we are back again for a few days. You will have read full accounts about the fighting at High Wood. It has been a great victory, but the cost was and is too much to bear. We are without nine hundred men and over who were here on the 12th Sunday after Trinity. They all went 'there' bravely and up to the last calmly cheerful. Some Battalions are worse off even than the poor 19th. Still, the Colonel, and 9 other officers out of 14—gone!

Yes, we lost our dear Colonel and 9 other officers out of the 14 that went. Several of them had their last Communion with me in the trenches, not the front line, just before the battle. Among others was the brave Lieut. Provand who went over with a little sprig of white heather which I gave him. It brought him no worldly luck, but it symbolised Scotland and honour and home, and I daresay all goes well with his noble soul. I sent the letter he gave me to his parents as I did for others also.

No words can tell you all I feel, nor can words tell you of the horrors of the clearing of a battlefield. This Battalion was left to do that, and several men went off with shell shock and two were wounded. I am certain the shell shock was caused not just by the explosion of a shell near by, but by the sights and smell and horror of the battlefield in general. I felt dreadful, and had to do my best to keep the men up to the task. When you stand over the body of a man whom you know, and lift the body on to a stretcher . . .

A letter comes to Major Fair saying that another officer, Lieut. Tyler of the 19th, has just died of wounds. So that makes 11 officers killed out of the 14 that went over. I wonder how the other 3 will fare? As I write another letter arrives saying another private has died of wounds, i.e. the 78th, and so it goes on.

The other day I lost the 19th and wandered about in front of High Wood and to the left of it. I found two German bayonets and also found an emblem worth all the German trophies put together. I enclose it. The Black Watch hackle. I wonder who wore this? Scotland for ever! All unknown to themselves they are the fiercest and best fighters for freedom and humanity on this earth.

25 September. All goes well. We have just been re-viewed by our General Macdow. It was the first inspec-tion since the battle of High Wood. It was on the training ground where they had all practised before the 15th. How inexpressibly sad to realise that hundreds upon hundreds of officers and men who were with this Brigade at the beginning are no more here by reason of Loos and High Wood. Still it is a fact that no more valuable victory has so far been won on the British side after the retreat of the Tyrant from Paris. It is an honour to be here.

Of course we Chaplains do little compared to the other

officers. Some do more than others, and some do get into a few of the danger zones with the men. I met a lonely New Zealand padre in a shell hole beyond High Wood. He was up burying some of his bonny lads. There is only one Front here and few Chaplains ever get there, and then not during engagements. It is a mistake on the part of the authorities which will cost the Church dearly. I have told my Seniors so, but law is law, in the Army as well as out of it.

(Note: Railton was apparently unaware that Army policy had by now changed. Padres were allowed to move freely at the front and to accompany their units into the line if desired. A number of padres were killed during the Battle of the Somme and others, like him, were decorated or commended for bravery.)

28 September. We are 'there' again, think of our poor lads up against it all once more. New drafts have come out but God alone knows what they are worth. We had a fearful long march yesterday. The day before I went to Amiens. I take it we may mention this far distant place as we are allowed to send cards of it. It is the first civilised place in which I have been for ages . . .

1 October. A fearful fight is proceeding. We have just had a transport service. I shall go up to the dressing station shortly, it is all terrible. Last night in Divisional Orders the M.C. was awarded to one of our Lieuts. Today he is killed.

I enclose the letter of the wife of Colonel Hamilton. I am glad I did as she wished, because I did not know. I found his body all alone, I cut off rank badges, buttons etc., all except the M.C. ribbon which he had won at Loos. The letter is an instance of the intense gratitude for small things which these people display to us padres.

Last night the 18th and 19th transport were shelled. Three men were wounded and seven horses hit. This morning at 1 a.m. I was coming back from the dressing station through the transport lines. I had a flashlight and I turned it on the wounded horses. One had a great hole all stopped up with wadding, the next had a hole in the head, the next in the legs and body, and so it went on. The flashlight showed up enough to tell me how terribly they had been wounded in taking food up to our men. But all was silent. Only one was breathing a little heavily, that was all.

I had just come from a dressing station. Our men suffer very bravely. But if you went into a dressing station after a battle blindfolded you would know at once from occasional groans and expressions and movements that men were there in pain. If you went through our transport lines blindfolded you would not have known that seven of our horses were wounded, for they suffer in absolute silence.

4 October. A great deal has happened since Sunday. Our men have been over the bags again and again. At first success was delayed but victory is here again. I have hardly time to relate it all now, but on Monday a Captain Clarke was killed by my side, or strictly a few paces behind me, and four others were wounded. God alone knows how I was missed. Of course this kind of thing happens constantly among officers and men of the Army, but as a rule our padre paths are freer of it.

Will you please send me an electric torch with a refill as life here at night is nothing more than pitch and toss. Every yard of ground here has been reconquered from the Boche. It is literally in parts, such as round High Wood, like a sea heaving in anger. Only it is different—as if the sea arose in anger, and then suddenly stood still. So when you go for a stroll over the 'sea' without a light, you get on top of a billow, the next moment you are clutching earth, and probably sucking it into your mouth in the deep trough of this 'sea', commonly called a shell-hole . . .

5 October. The Brigade is 'out'. There have been a few blunders but on the whole it has done extremely well. The Boche still retires.

I hear that the vile villain who killed Captain Clarke the doctor, and wounded four others of our 'wounded' party, was in a tank. This tank had been discarded and burnt by our men after the advance. The Boche sniper knew we were a stretcher-party, as the men carried their stretchers over their shoulders. He also boasted when he was captured that he had shot 15 officers. Such are the unsporting, low brutes that are too often opposed to us.

Of course it is not every German that I loathe, but the German spirit is of the Devil, it is hell poison. Indeed, I try to act justly by them, and so do the others. I have seen our men give the Boche water out of their own water-bottles. I have given them food and drink myself when others looked on as much as to say, 'Why bother about the devils?' The night before last I conducted a young wounded Boche officer to the ambulance across the end of High Wood. I treated him as gently as if he were an Englishman. He is 18 and won the Iron Cross a month ago.

He told me the Boche could afford to lose ground as 'we gained so much at the beginning of the war.' He spoke in German, I asked him to do so partly out of interest and also because his loud-voiced optimism might have been heard by our men and enraged them. He said they had plenty of men! Our stretcher-bearers were carrying a man in front of us and shells were falling in the distance. Suddenly one fell near. Down went all the stretcher-bearers! I crouched down but did not let my wounded Boche go; he remained standing erect. When it all ceased he said in broken English, 'The German artillery falls badly.' He explained to me that he meant their shooting was bad. I was amused at his gibe at his own artillery when he himself would have been a victim of that shell if it had fallen a little more accurately.

He was the first optimistic Boche we had met on our sector. He is young. I hope he will live to see the three sacred aims of this war gained:

1. Germany forfeit all land outside Germany.

2. Germany pay war indemnity.

3. Germany forbidden to have an army or navy.

Ah! if only it should come true. At least our children would never know the horror of war. God help us to victory, and if it so please Him, use us as His mighty avengers by and by up and down the length and breadth of Germany.

I must write to Mrs Clarke, whose noble husband was shot just behind me, by that low skunk of a creature. Hence three little children mourn a noble father, not to mention his poor wife. Uptil recently I encouraged and urged marriage during the war; never, never, never again. No, I would rather make a man, if I could, break off his engagement and never write again than that he married till this is over. Even if men have been engaged for years, let them wait or break it off. On no account marry. It is more than cruel to the wives and children, it is agony to the men, often they have told me so.

Half the men do not fear death or wounds. I don't fear death as death, but I dread even a wound for the anxiety it may give to you. I should mourn the death of a man like Clarke if he were single, and I should loathe the treacherous devil who shot him. But I mourn in fifty-fold agony and loathe with a thousand-fold ferocity when I think of Mrs Clarke and those three tiny ones. I promised to marry several of our officers, if they liked during the war. Now I shall refuse to do it, and I hope every Vicar they meet will do his best to prevent it. They can still be lovers and wait. At the end of the war, if he lives, they will receive their reward in the joy-life of marriage.

Our men have just brought in some of the captured. It is odd to see a man in khaki with a new Boche helmet on his head or a grey coat over his shoulder, but I say 'Hurrah! hurrah! hurrah!' inwardly whenever I see it.

6 October. Our casualty lists are terrible! One battalion went up with 700 on Saturday and it has come back with 200. God help us all . . .

8 October . . . I can barely keep my eyes open as I write. In the middle of reading I fell asleep for a moment, and this morning I dropped a prayer-book into the mud of the trenches. I am very well, it is just natural tiredness . . .

11 October. We are out of the line. A report comes this morning that they are going to take our remnants back by train. Dear lads—if it were true! Fancy a train! a real puffer! a lift for a good ten miles or so! I wonder!

I enclose another typical letter of gratitude. Capt. David Henderson was killed in High Wood. He is the son of Arthur Henderson M.P. who was Leader of the Labour Party in Parliament, was till recently President of the Board of Education and is now Paymaster General. The letter is written by a brother of David Henderson, with whom I was very pally. The day before battle, when I had a Celebration, Henderson lent me his dug-out. He could not come himself. He was brought up a Nonconformist but he said towards the end of a drill, 'The Padre is going to have a Celebration of Holy Communion, if there are any volunteers for it, they can fall out.'

Eight men of that lot came. It was so odd to hear them

called volunteers for Communion, but yet the phrase is natural. They are all volunteers—in that sacred matter. Ah, the men—grand young men we have lost! Ask the Vicar please from me—to pray always at Celebrations —to give it out—for the relatives of men who have been killed. Do we realise their agonies? Germany's crime will last—deeply in the hearts and minds at least of our children . . .

Shortly afterwards Railton went home on leave. A surprise awaited his return:

Last night when I arrived the transport officer (Maclagan) greeted me with 'Many congratulations, Padre.' I said I had luckily escaped all the traps of the Boche —submarines, mines etc. 'No,' he said, 'M.C.' I replied, 'Well, I knew you would have some joke, old Mac.' 'No, it's no joke, it came out in Orders last night.'

I then went up the line with the transport. Fair and all the others greeted me the same way, and Fair actually pinned the Military Cross ribbon on. I took it off saying, 'Well, I must wait until it is gazetted.' 'No, you musn't,' said Fair, 'put it on at once, it was sent for you from Headquarters.'

Well, it is a strange fact. Why I have received the honour I do not know. I suppose it must be for High Wood or the Clarke affair. God alone knows how little I deserve it compared to many of our combatant officers and men. And yet they seem to be really pleased that I have got it . . .

In a letter written the following day Railton appears torn between delight and misgiving at the acclaim triggered off by the decoration. The quandary he hints at was the quandary that faced any padre with a real sense of mission—how far to court popularity, avoiding any semblance of a holier-than-thou attitude, in order to get through to the irreligious and exert an influence for good.

. . . Last night an officer, a Scot in the front line, gave me a most terrific grip of the hand and said, 'Congratulations Padre, you d—— well deserve it.' Funny way to congratulate a Padre, but it was meant. As a matter of fact I am half ashamed to wear the ribbon. I know dozens of men who hourly hazard their lives and have nothing by way of reward.

Oh, they are great and splendid, just think of their jovial ways! A Major who swears and tells dirty tales—a real genuine man—always his real self, Padre present or absent—looked me straight in the face and said, 'Padre, next to the old man (i.e. the devil) I love you best in the regiment!' His way of showing affection. He is not such a bad lot as he makes out. He is a fine man. What I would not do to be able to win such a man out and out for the great Master.

I would prefer to be downright. I could reprove with a look or a word, but often I see the fact that all our clerical ways have upset so many of these men. Hence they don't follow our Lord. If a Padre looks reproof when they say or do wrong, they feel, 'Ah—sanctimonious, superior —aloof—inhuman priest.' If I say nothing they say, 'The Padre is a sport.' Of course it does not matter what they say, but it does matter whether they withdraw and get politely aloof, and never heed a word you say or come for advice. This is what often happens, God help me through His Holy Spirit.

As I write they are playing at cards for money. One officer said aloud to attract my attention, 'Padre's shocked! Never mind, he is a sport.' I am in a mood at present wherein I am tired of the war. Tired of seeing wounds and death and mud and filth, and yet conscious that the earth can never be peaceful until the Boche is crushed and out of the way of humanity. Oh, what a grouse! and probably in ten minutes I shall be laughing with the others.

During the agonisingly cold winter months ahead ('Oh the fierce terrible winter! what a ghastly, awful thing, the winter!') Railton was to refer on a number of occasions to the need for keeping up a cheerful front, even at times when he felt at such a low ebb that he could admit to understanding how men in the 'untold Hell of the trenches' could be driven to blaspheme. That he had by now gained a reputation for cheerfulness is apparent from one reference to having overheard an officer in his billet describing him to a French girl as 'a true comrade to us, who has won a medal and is "toujours gai"'.

In one of the last of his letters to have been preserved, written in March 1917 on the Ypres front, Railton sums up the lessons he has learned as a padre and which he sees as equally applicable to the home front. One wonders how much his insistence on the need for 'merry, joyful Christians' in order to 'win men to the Banner of Jesus Christ' was inspired by memories of that Army his father had helped to lead to conquests around the world, marching through shabby streets to the sound of trumpets and drums and tambourines and the rousing exhortations of 'Onward Christian Soldiers'.

I have at last found the way to convert any country to our Lord. Let every churchman be always cheerful and always hopeful. The rest of mankind will want to know why it is that the churchman is always more cheerful than anybody else. This is not the case now.

Our Army is renowned for its cheery ways. Let the Church get the same reputation tenfold. As it is, other professions shine more—whatever their trials may be.

[73]

The actor or actress or singer comes on the stage smiling. The clergyman goes into the pulpit looking—bored —sad—soft—or poisoned. The layman often comes away from the theatre full of smiles. He, or she, too often comes away from Communion looking like the Boche do when they surrender to our men. In fact the Boche often looks more pleased. Let the communicant come away from church radiant. They do occasionally —certainly out here. A C.S.M. told me last week he noticed how specially calm and happy they looked just before going 'over the bags'—after they had received their Communion.

Compare a platform of politicians and one of black-garbed clergy. The former so often look victory. We look defeat. A Church Congress, a Mother's Meeting, a Men's Society Gathering, religious drawing-room affairs or Communicants' Guilds, look at least as solemn and dull as a herd of cows. The only advantage is with the cows—they do look natural and content.

Oh! that we could shake ourselves at once. I am sure that I have found the cure. Always be—at least outwardly—Bright. If every churchman was always as bright as an officers' mess here—our churches would be over-filled and grand work done.

Railton, who was killed in a railway accident in 1955 at the age of 70, never forgot the lessons he had learned as a padre on the Western Front. Though his hopes of a 'new era' of religion after the war were far from being realised, his own ministry was marked by a rare ability to fill churches. And of equal importance to him was the rapport he was able to establish with those who never darkened the door of a church, many of them ex-servicemen who had found no 'land fit for heroes' on their return from the trenches, but unemployment, poverty and hunger.

Railton's son Andrew, born in 1920, recalls his father as 'a remarkable man, not at all clever in an intellectual sense, but a magnetic personality, popular with everyone.' He was aware, however, that popularity was not what his father sought, and that he was always disturbingly conscious of the great gap that existed between the established churches and the great mass of people.

'He was torn apart between an establishment respect for authority and an urge, inherited from his father, for street corner evangelism, unconnected with any church,' says Andrew Railton. 'About the time of the General Strike he gave up a comfortable living to work for two years for the Industrial Christian Fellowship.'

One of Railton's earliest newspaper records of his father, when Vicar of Margate, is of the three months he spent disguised as a tramp, living a vagrant's life from hand to mouth, sleeping in doss-houses, discovering what it was like to be down-and-out. 'He had great sympathy and understanding for those in distress. Though he rarely talked about his war years as a padre, there is no doubt that his experiences in the trenches had had a profound effect on him. As a parish priest he devoted much time to visiting his poorer parishioners, not to get them to church, but to bring them hope and encouragement.'

In the pulpit Railton practised what he had preached in those letters to his wife urging the need for 'merry, joyful Christians'. 'As a boy I can remember queues outside the church when my father was to preach,' his son recalls.

He was a natural orator, with a touch of the actor in him, never boring. He could put over the simple Gospel story in a most compelling way, always with a message of hope. He had no time for what he called the 'holy women' of the church—the high church type of priest with his genuflections, intonings and holier-than-thou aura. If he had a fault it was that his own faith was so deep-rooted and unshakeable that he found it hard to understand those who could not share it.

Railton had served as Vicar at Folkestone, Margate, Bradford and Bolton, and Shalford in Surrey, before being appointed to his last living, as Rector of Liverpool. There he came closest to courting unpopularity in the stand he made against the introduction of football pools. 'My grandfather would have greatly approved the stormy open-air meetings he conducted', says Andrew Railton. 'They thought gambling evil because it could mean wives and kids going hungry.'

During the Second World War, when Railton's waterfront church was gutted in an air raid, he found an unexpected outlet for his 'God on our side' patriotism, as an 'Archbishop's visitor' to the RAF. Archbishop Temple appointed six senior clergymen to visit RAF stations around the country, taking services and boosting the morale of the RAF chaplains.

After the war Railton retired with his wife to a village near Fort William in the West Highlands of Scotland, a country for which he had always had a romantic leaning. But he continued to preach right up to his death. Among clergy friends in many parts of the United Kingdom he was in great demand as a 'locum' during their absence on holiday. Locally he incurred the displeasure of an Episcopalian bishop by preaching in Presbyterian as well as Church of Scotland pulpits. But ecumenicalism had come a long way since he had first seen it as a hope for the future of religion. Four Roman Catholic priests were among the interdenominational friends at his funeral, mourning a man who had long ago discovered that it did not greatly matter whether a Christian was 'High or Low, Broad or Catholic, or a Dissenter, whether he gives allegiance to Canterbury, Rome or to General Booth'.

It is by a grave not his own, one of the most visited graves in the country, that Railton would have wished to be remembered. The 'inspiration' that came to him one day at the front in 1916 and which eventually led to the ceremonial reburial of the remains of an 'unknown warrior' in Westminster Abbey, was one he regarded as God-given, and which is certainly a noteable example of the religious mystique surrounding the war. No spot is deemed more hallowed in our National Shrine than this last resting place of a man who, for all that anyone can know, may not have believed in the existence of God at all.

In an article on 'The Origin of the Unknown Warrior's Grave', written by Railton in 1931 'at the request of the Editor' of a magazine called *Our Empire*, he emotionally recalls the genesis of the idea.

I came back from 'the line' at dusk. We had just laid to rest the mortal remains of a comrade. I went to the billet in front of Erkingham, near Armentières. At the back of the billet was a small garden, and in the garden, only about six paces from the house, there was a grave. At the head of the grave there stood a rough cross of white wood. On the cross was written in deep black-pencilled letters, 'An Unknown British Soldier', and in brackets underneath, 'of the Black Watch'.

It was dusk, and no one was near, except some officers in the billet playing cards. I remember how still it was. Even the guns seemed to be resting. How that grave gave me to think! How I wondered! How I longed to see his folk! But, who was he, and who were they? . . . Quietly and gradually there came out of the mist of thought this answer, clear and strong, 'Let this body—this symbol of him—be carried reverently over the sea to his native land.' . . .

It was not until August 1920 that Railton wrote to the Dean of Westminster, Bishop Herbert Ryle, with the suggestion that an unknown soldier should be buried among the nation's 'illustrious dead' in the Abbey. A committee was set up, which recommended that the Foreign Minister should take immediate steps to make a body available for the forth-coming Armistice Day celebrations, on 11 November, when King George V was to unveil the Cenotaph in Whitehall.

Rarely can there have been such a macabre admixture of military pomp and religious fervour as in the events that followed. To ensure that identification would be impossible, four bodies were dug up in the four main battle areas of the Western Front (the Aisne, the Somme, Arras and Ypres) and brought to the military cemetery chapel at St Pol (near the site of the battle of Agincourt). They were placed on stretchers in a row in front of the altar, each draped with a Union Jack. At midnight on 7–8 November a Brigadier-General selected one, which was placed in a coffin brought from England (the other three bodies were later buried in the cemetery).

In the morning Anglican, Roman Catholic and Noncon-formist padres joined forces in a service, after which the body was sent under escort to Boulogne. From then on it was a half-triumphant, half-reverential progress, by destroyer to Dover, by train to Victoria (in the carriage that had brought home the body of Nurse Cavell), finally through silent crowds to the Cenotaph, the coffin resting on a gun-carriage flanked by Top Brass of the three services, including Earl Haig.

From the Cenotaph the King led the procession to the Abbey. During the service the elite of the land listened with emotion to the high-sounding phrases: 'They buried him among Kings, because he had done good towards God, and towards His house . . .' The music was by English com-posers, and included Kipling's Recessional. During the sing-ing of 'Lead Kindly Light' the bearers removed the helmet and side-arms from the coffin and lowered it into the tomb.

At the commital the King scattered earth brought from the battlefields. Drums rolled, the Last Post rang out, followed by the Reveille. Finally 100 holders of the Victoria Cross led the file past on either side of the tomb. After such a ceremony, it was perhaps surprising that the words chosen to be inscribed on the stone over the tomb should have been so restrained, invoking neither God, King nor Country: 'Thus are commemorated the many multitudes who gave the most that men can give.'

For Railton it had been the Union Jack used in the Abbey that day that held the most poignant memories. He had suggested to Dean Ryle that 'a real "War" flag in my possession should be used at the burial, rather than a new flag of no "service" experience', and the Dean had agreed. The flag he had once described in a letter to his wife as a 'symbol of Christ' had now become the symbol of a nation's tribute and mourning. Railton wrote:

The flag had been used during the war at Holy Communion, as a covering for the rough box, or table, Altars. It was used at Church Parades and Ceremonial Parades. It was the covering—often the only covering—of the slain, as their bodies were laid to rest. For all I know it may have been used in Belgium or France when the actual 'Unknown Warrior' was slain. It was not a new 'bit of bunting', bought for the occasion, but a real symbol of every Briton's life. Indeed, it is literally tinged with the life-blood of fellow Britons.

A year after the dedication of the Unknown Warrior's tomb, Railton was himself present at another, little publicised, ceremony in the Abbey. He watched with emotion as a squad of a battalion in which he had served placed his flag on a pillar near the tomb: the flag he had never doubted had been synonymous with the 'banner of our Lord', leading Christian soldiers to victory against the fiends. It hangs there to this day.

CHAPTER THREE

CROSS AGAINST CRESCENT

'Now, boys, you're not over-religious, I expect, but you're Christians before you're Moslems, and your hands should fly to your swords when I say the Gallipoli campaign is a New Crusade . . . It's the Cross against the Crescent again. By Jove, it's splendid, perfectly splendid! And an English cross, too!' . . .

It was with such pious exhortations that the Colonel in Ernest Raymond's semi-autobiographical novel, *Tell England*, sought to inspire his young officers on the eve of their embarkation for the 'Great Adventure', the death struggle against the Turks on the barren and rugged Gallipoli Peninsula that had so fired the popular imagination since the first British troops had stormed its beaches, under a murderous hail of bullets, on 25 April 1915.

No campaign in the First World War had a more potent religious appeal. Its ultimate aim was the capture of Constantinople, the only ancient city purely Christian in origin, which had been built by the Emperor Constantine in honour of the Virgin Mary, but which for centuries had been in the hands of the infidel. And older religions than Christianity loomed in the background.

The Gallipoli section of Raymond's novel is irradiated

with romantic allusions to those battles long ago in which the pagan gods had played such an active and conflicting role. For it was across Homer's 'wine-dark seas', now patrolled by battleships of the Royal Navy, that Agamemnon's thousand ships had brought his Greek warriors to lay siege to Troy. Across the Dardanelles (the ancient Hellespont, where later Darius and Xerxes were to pour their invading Persians across bridges of boats), one could see above the Troad plain the summit of Mount Ida from which Zeus had gazed down on the conflict. From the blue Aegean rose the hazy outlines of Samothrace, where Poseidon, god of the sea, had kept watch, and the island of Lemnos, where Vulcan in his smithy had forged the weapons of Achilles.

Few campaigns have been more written about than the 8-months-long Gallipoli campaign, which Churchill had seen as 'the shortest path to a triumphant peace', but which ended with an ignominious evacuation and an estimated 265,000 Allied casualties, of whom some 46,000 were killed or died of wounds or sickness. But no factual accounts have had as great an impact as *Tell England*, an instant best-seller when published in 1922, reprinted numerous times since, and still in steady demand in public libraries.

For the purposes of this book the Gallipoli section of *Tell England* is of valid interest in that the central character in it is a Church of England padre, and that it is based on Raymond's own experiences as a padre during the closing stages of the campaign. In this chapter it will be compared with a journal, recently come to light, written by a curate who, by choice, served as a private in the Royal Army Medical Corps at Gallipoli, and who has a very different story to tell.

It was during Raymond's four years as a padre in various theatres of war that he wrote the latter part of *Tell England* (surreptitiously, in field service notebooks), basing the Galli-poli chapters on the diary he had kept there. After its publication in 1922, as he reveals in his autobiography, he was amazed at the extreme reactions it aroused. Some critics, including Rose Macaulay and Alec Waugh, slated it— 'sloppy, sentimental and in bad taste', 'laughable when it is not revolting by reason of its sticky sentimentality', 'the most nauseating book to come out of the war'. Most were enthusiastic, notably Hannen Swaffer who hailed it as 'a great book . . . a book of penetrating analysis . . . a book that will live as long as our spoken tongue'.

Raymond himself admitted that, rereading it after fifty years, parts of it made him 'shiver', but he had no reservations about the 'overspill of pieties and spiritual uplift'. And there can be little doubt that his portrait of Padre Monty, the 'spare, lean and vigorous' High Churchman, with his talk of war as a crusade and of eve-of-battle confessions and celebrations of mass that would 'send you into the fight—white', was an idealised version of what he had aspired to be. Ludicrously high-flown as Padre Monty's effusions must read today, their sentiments were common enough currency in the euphoric early stages of the war, whether in pulpits or in the outpourings of soldier-poets like Rupert Brooke: 'Now God be thanked who has matched us with His hour . . .'

In most padres' accounts of their experiences at the front, there is a tendency to concentrate on events and to take for granted the spiritual aspects of their ministrations. Raymond is no exception. Religion scarcely figures in the section of his autobiography covering his years as a padre. But in the ostensibly fictional *Tell England* he could let himself go, without inhibition. And that Padre Monty expressed his own beliefs seems clear from earlier references to his own conversion. It was during his last year at school that he had caught from a friend 'the splendid fever of the Anglo-Catholic movement, with all its beauties of ceremonial and worship, which at that date was capturing the imagination of so many young men.'

Shortly after his first appointment as a curate in 1915, at the age of 27, Raymond offered his services as a padre. There is a revealing glimpse in his autobiography of the ease with which a fit young clergyman could turn padre in his description of the day he went to the War Office, armed with a recommendation from his vicar, to be interviewed by the Chaplain-General.

. . . Bishop Taylor Smith, whose manner is brisk and brusque, as though he would say, 'There's a war on, and no time to waste', shoots at me a fusillade of questions. Most of the questions I answer well enough, but the last one foolishly. Thus:

Bishop (a low churchman): 'What would you do if a soldier came to you and said he was tired of his sins and wanted to be a Christian?'

E.R. (Determined to be loyal to his Anglo-Catholicity, even if it cost all): 'I should tell him to come and make his confession.'

Bishop: 'Wouldn't understand what you're talking about. Go down to the M.O.'s and see if you're fit for service abroad . . .'

There were seven other young chaplains (including the Rev. William Wand, a future Bishop of London) aboard the troopship *Scotian* in which Raymond sailed for the Mediterranean in July 1915. In *Tell England* Padre Monty appears to have had to himself the run of the similarly crowded troopship *Rangoon*, and to have lost no time in initiating daily pre-breakfast masses in the smoking room, 'with a little altar that supported two lighted candles', and in gaining the confidences of the more likely looking of the young officers.

Rupert Ray and Edgar Doe, the two public school chums of the earlier chapters, readily succumb to the bluff charm of this dog-collared eccentric, who has already seen service on the Western Front, has taken the measure of the 'horrible, pink Huns, with their round heads, cropped hair and large necks', and found the Tommy, however bad his language, to be 'the most lovable creature in the world'.

A few excerpts will suffice to show how the irrepressible Monty, who had soon formed a dozen subalterns into a guild of servers for early mass, talked his way through the defences of the two high-spirited heroes and brought them to the realisation that war could be ennobling and death (for God, King and Country) the greatest adventure of all. His homilies, punctuated with a good deal of whimsical chaff, were usually delivered after dinner as the three reclined in deck chairs under the stars on the blacked-out boat deck.

. . . 'I know the sort of religion you've enjoyed—and, for that matter, adorned', said Monty. 'It's a wonderful creed! Have a bath every morning and go to church with your people. It saves you from bad form, but can't save you from vice.'

Doe moved slightly in his chair, as one does when a dentist touches a nerve . . .

. . . 'And what are we to believe about the Mass?' asked Doe, who, deeply interested, had turned his chair towards Monty.

Monty told us. He told us things strange for us to hear. We were to believe that the bread and wine, after consecration, were the same Holy Thing as the Babe of Bethlehem; and we could come to Mass, not to partake, but to worship like the shepherds and the Magi; and there, and there only, should we learn how to worship. He told us that the Mass was the most dramatic service in the world, for it was the acting before God of Calvary's ancient sacrifice; and under the shadow of that sacrifice we could pray out all our longings and all our loneliness . . .

. . . 'You boys are born hero-worshippers,' Monty said. 'And there's nothing that warm young blood likes better than to do homage to its hero, and mould itself on its hero's lines. In the Mass you simply bow the knee to your Hero, and say: "I swear fealty. I'm going to mould myself on you."'

He had not known Edgar Doe forty-eight hours, but he had his measure.

'All right' said Doe. 'I'll come.'

'Tell us about the other thing, confession,' I suggested.

'Not now, Rupert. "Ye are babes," and I've fed you with milk. Confession'll come, but it's strong meat for you yet.' . . .

'. . . Oh, I admit I'm out to win you two. I want to prove that the old Church of England has everything you public schoolboys need, and capture you and hold you. I want all the young blood for her. I want to prove that you can be the pride of the Church of England. And I'll prove it. I'll prove it on this ship.' . . .

. . . One immortal Friday fully forty wandered in to Mass. Monty was radiant. Immediately after the service he said to me: 'Come on deck, and have a game of quoits-tennis before breakfast. Mass first, then tennis —that's as it should be.' We went on deck, and, having fixed the rope that acted as a net, played a hard game. And, when the first game was finished, Monty, still flushed with his victory in the smoking room, came and looked at me over the high intervening rope, much as a horse looks over a wall, and proceeded to hold forth:

'D'you remember that picture, "The Vigil", Rupert, where a knight is kneeling with his sword before the altar, being consecrated for the work he has in hand? Well, this voyage is the vigil for these fellows. Before they step ashore, they shall kneel in front of the same altar, and seek a blessing on their swords. Hang it! aren't they young knights setting out on perilous work? And I'll prove we have a church still, and an Altar, and a Vigil.'

Then he asked me what I was stopping for and talking about, and why I didn't get on with the game. His spirits were irrepressible . . .

. . . 'Tell us about confession,' I said, and curled myself up to listen.

'Right,' agreed Monty.

'But wait,' warned Doe. 'You're not going to get me to come to confession. I value your good opinion too highly.'

'My dear Gazelle, don't be absurd. I'll have you promise tonight.'

'You won't!'

'I will! Here goes . . .'

. . . 'The two cardinal dogmas of my faith are—'

'The Mass and confession,' I volunteered, in a flash of impudence.

'Don't interrupt, you rude little cub. They are these. Just as there is more beauty in nature than ugliness, so there is more goodness in humanity than evil, and more happiness in the world than sorrow . . . It's my task to make this voyage your Vigil; and a perfect Vigil. It's all inexpressibly dear to me. I'm going to send you down that gangway when you go ashore to this crusade— properly absolved by your Church. I'm going to send you into the fight—*white*.'

. . . Monty's cabin was to be his confessional. I was to go to him early the next morning, as I had been detailed for Submarine Watch for the remainder of the day.

I approached his door, stimulating myself for the ordeal by saying 'In half an hour I shall have told all, and the thing will be done.' A certain happiness fought in my mind against my shrinking from self-humiliation.

I found Monty ready for me, robed in a surplice and violet stole. In front of the place where I was to kneel was a crucifix.

'Kneel there,' said Monty, 'and, if necessary, look at that. *He* was so much a man like us that He kept the glory that was set before Him as a motive for enduring the cross.' . . .

Did anything like all this actually happen? In his autobiography Raymond gives no indication as to what extent Monty's crusading activities are based on his own experiences as an Anglo-Catholic padre in theatres of war as diverse as Gallipoli, Sinai, Mesopotamia, Ypres and Russia. After the war he was to lose his faith and leave the church to become a full-time writer. But one must assume that his faith was as strong as ever during the three months he spent on the Gallipoli Peninsula up to the evacuation, and that the chapters in *Tell England* covering the same period are to some extent realistic.

For Ray and Doe it must have been hard to sustain those visions Monty had conjured up of a holy crusade, of knights brandishing their consecrated swords. In the stalemate of trench warfare that had set in, death was a desultory affair of shellbursts and snipers' bullets, disease and the elements were a common enemy. The 'death or glory' days had passed, and it was in a reflective mood that the two one day visited the beaches of Cape Helles, 'thinking of the British Army that blew in one day like a gale from the sea'. On the headland they see the old trenches and gun positions, the scattered cemeteries and solitary graves, on one of which is inscribed: 'Tell England, ye who pass this monument/We died for her, and here we rest content.'

But both still cling to Monty's conception of war as ennobling. They even take in their stride their CO's exhortation on arrival: 'You mustn't rest till you've slaughtered a Turk.

Then, if they kill you, you'll at least have taken a life for a life. And any more that you kill before they finish you off will be clear gain for King George.' Before long each has accounted for an unwary Turk the other side of no-man's-land.

Occasionally Monty invites them into his dugout, over-looking the Aegean Sea, for tea and a chin-wag. But he is not present when Doe one night confides in his friend what amounts to a death-wish. It would have been revealing to have learned how far that 'masterly priest' could have approved the sentiments. (The French phrases are expressive of Doe's current addiction to French literature.)

. . . 'Yes, Roop, living through war is living deep. It's crowded, glorious living. If I'd never had a shell rush at me I'd never have known the swift thrill of approaching death—which is a sensation not to be missed. If I'd never known the shock of seeing sudden death at my side, I'd have missed a terribly wonderful thing. They say music's the most evocative art in the world, but sacre nom de Dieu, they hadn't counted on the orchestra of a bombard-ment. That's music at ten thousand pounds a minute. And if I'd not heard that, I'd never have known what it is to have my soul drawn out of me by the maddening excitement of an intensive bombardment. And—and, que voulez-vous, I have *killed*!'

'Hm!' muttered I. He was too clever for me, but I loved him in his scintillating moments.

'Tiens, if I'm knocked out, it's at least the most wonderful death. It's the *deepest* death.' . . .

It is on the night before Doe is killed, leading a raid into enemy lines to silence a troublesome gun, that Monty at last comes into his own again. He visits his two favourite con-verts in their dugout and is soon bringing the conversation round to his shipboard homilies.

'Since those days you've been fairly loyal sons of the Church. Aren't you going to use her before tomorrow? Tonight's a more literal Vigil than that voyage. Can't I—aren't you going to use me?'

It was the old Monty of the Rangoon speaking.

'We'd thought about it,' answered Doe, reddening.

'I so want,' murmured Monty, 'to be of use to all the fellows who are going over the top tomorrow. But they don't understand. They don't think of me as a priest with something to do for them that nobody else can do. They think I've done my job when I've had a hymn-singing service, and preached to them. And all the time I want to absolve them. I want to send them into the fight—white.'

No word came from us to break a long pause. We had become again those listening people of Rangoon nights.

'But *you* understand,' he recommenced. 'And, if you'll come to your Confession, I'll at least have done something for somebody before this scrap. Rupert, you can thank Heaven you don't feel as I do—that you've nothing positive to do tomorrow—that you're not pulling your weight. I shall just skulk about, like a dog worrying the heels of an attack.'

'Rot!' said Doe. 'You've done wonders for the men.'

'No, I haven't, except for those who come to their Mass and Confession. I've held no services a layman couldn't hold, and done nothing for the sick a hospital orderly couldn't do. And I want to be their priest.'

'Well, we'll both come tonight.'

Monty ceased frowning at the sea, and smilingly turned towards us.

'You may think,' he said, 'that I've been of some help to you; but you can never know what help you two have been to me.'

'Oh, rot!' said Doe, tossing a pencil in the air . . .

[89]

The reader is left to conjecture what spiritual succour Padre Monty was able to provide, or what succour he received, at the bedside of the mortally wounded Doe next day. Ray, after a stiff-upper-lip farewell to his friend, had rushed away from the hospital tent, 'with an audible moan', leaving the two together.

But later, when Monty seeks to comfort Ray, there is a noteable absence of Christian dogma in his reflections on death. In none of his homilies, indeed, has he spoken of a reward for sacrifice, of a life to come, of a resurrection, let alone of the hell and purgatory proclaimed by the Roman Catholic Church. Now, as the grief-stricken Ray hints that his friend's 'unbeautiful' death has shaken his belief in all that Monty has instilled into him, one might have expected him to come out with a resounding reassurance—of the trumpets sounding for Doe on the other side, of a crown of glory. Instead, apart from the vague reference to a divine spark 'escaping away', his final words on the Holy Crusade could almost be those of a humanist, applicable alike to Christian and infidel, Cross and Crescent.

. . . Both of us watched the sun going down behind Imbros. It was throwing out golden rays like the spokes of a wheel. These rays caught the flaky clouds above Samothrace, and just pencilled their outline with a tiny rim of gold and fire. And the hills of Imbros, as always in the Aegean Sea, turned purple.

'There's no beauty in death and burial and corruption,' I said.

'Yes, there is, even in them. There's beauty in thinking that the same material which goes to make these earthly hills and that still water should have been shaped into a beautiful body, and lit with the divine spark which was Edgar Doe. There's beauty in thinking that, when the unconquerable spark has escaped away, the material is returned to the earth, where it urges its life, also an unconquerable thing, into grass and flowers. It's harmonious—it's beautiful.' . . .

Like Ernest Raymond, Harold Augustine Thomas served at Gallipoli during the closing stages of the campaign, and like him kept a diary of his experiences. But the down-to-earth journal he wrote from it could be in a different world from the officer-orientated, romanticised Gallipoli of *Tell England*.

The journal's chief interest lies in the fact that Thomas, a curate like Raymond, could have volunteered as a padre, but had chosen instead to rough it as a private in the Royal Army Medical Corps. In his account there is little of the heroic in the gruelling activities of a stretcher-bearer among the dead and dying; his fellow-Tommies could scarcely be described as 'the most lovable creatures in the world'; and religion takes a back seat. Thomas's high hopes of conducting, in the guise of a Tommy, 'a missionary enterprise without parallel', appears to have met with as little success as Monty's burning desire to be 'of use as a priest'.

Born in 1883, son of a clergyman and eldest of a family of seven, Thomas won a scholarship to Lancing College and an exhibition to Jesus College, Oxford, where he studied the classics and English literature and gained B.A. and M.A. degrees. His decision to enlist, while a curate at Alsager in Cheshire, surprised everyone. By no means the extrovert, sporting type of cleric, he was noted as an eloquent preacher and a lover of music and poetry (his readings from Kipling and other favourite poets were popular in the parish).

Thomas's journal starts with the reasoning that led to his decision. On one side the bishops were urging that the clergy were most needed at home, his vicar was incapacitated by blindness from carrying on alone, and his fiancée was expecting to marry that autumn after a four years' engagement. On the other side was the challenge he had been putting to

himself, particularly after reading the despatches from Gallipoli in the papers—'What am I doing in this comfortable
place at the height of manhood, 32?'

. . . 'You daren't, you funk the rawness and discomfort
of it all,' I told myself. 'You know how you hated the
Cadet Corps at school and how you wriggled out of it on
the plea of extra work for a scholarship—you simply
daren't do it, you're too soft.' And then the picture of the
disagreeableness of the Tommy's life rose before me: the
crowdedness of it—the lack of privacy—the beastly
food—the infernal drills—the dirt of it and roughness of
it (how coarse some of my friends had grown after a few
weeks in the ranks): the more clearly this picture showed
before me the more convinced I began to feel that I *ought*
to go.

I am afraid the religious and priestly side of the question did not play a very large part in my verdict on
myself. But I think I saw at once what a gorgeous
opportunity was here afforded for the clergy to come into
real touch with the People—the men—the thousands of
them for whom not the Church only but the religion of
Jesus had ceased to exist. Here was a chance to get
amongst men whom the Church never sees except as
unconscious babes or inanimate corpses. Apart from the
justice of our Cause, it was a missionary enterprise
without parallel. The Nation had been caught in a fool's
paradise but the Nation was undoubtedly awakening.
The Church was also in a fool's paradise (still blindly
clinging to the belief that at heart she held the people) but,
unlike the Nation, the Church continued to sleep and the
majority of her Bishops encouraged her sleep. No! there
was no shred of excuse for hanging back on the religious
score . . .

Thomas found two other parsons, and several Salvation Army men, among the 60 'rookies' with whom he reported for duty, on 24 May 1915, at the headquarters of a Field Ambulance in the close of the cathedral city of Norwich. The transformation from curate, accustomed to deference, to put-upon Tommy was immediate. Though still in clerical garb during the first three weeks, he found himself acting as 'domestic servant' to a fussy officer, cleaning his equipment, making his bed, collecting his washing, cleaning his grate and laying the fire, scrubbing the floor and getting his meals ready. But when issued with khaki tunic, trousers, puttees and cap, he discovered, to his evident surprise and delight, 'the extraordinary change in personality which comes with uniform'.

Apart from the necessary uncongeniality of some of the tasks, the life, as compared with that of a working clergyman, was phenomenally lazy. It was at once a nerve-cure and a renewal of youth. Once the routine of drill had been mastered there was nothing to trouble about. Worry simply did not exist. To get down like this close to life gave a joy to living which I had lost since Ordination. As a clergyman every conversation had an ulterior motive, as a Tommy each individual and each conversation yielded its natural quota of instruction or amusement. Previously one had looked a little askance at Life, one had wondered whether it had infidel leanings or not. One worried about individuals, one worried about ideas, one worried about responsibilities. Now one worried about nothing.

It was like being at school again—astonishingly like it. The O.C. was the Head, the officers were the masters, the N.C.O.'s were the prefects and you were a fourth form boy and liable to fagging! It was great to feel one had the zest for such a life at 32! . . .

There were occasions during this training period when Thomas reverted briefly to his old status:

The C.O. would enquire of local clergy whether they required help on Sundays and intimated that he could supply their needs from the resources of the Ambulance, at the usual fee. Consequently I, with the other parson-privates, found myself detailed for preaching duties in the neighbourhood, the guineas resulting from such engagements being handed over to the O.C. for the benefit of the Corps and Band Fund. A notice would appear in Monday evening orders to the effect that the Corps had benefitted to the amount of certain guineas by the services of Private X! Finances military and musical received considerable increase from our willingly expended energies! Certainly it was a treat to return to social amenities if only for a fleeting Sabbath . . .

For Private Thomas, M.A., the most bizarre occasion was when he received written orders from 'our enterprising C.O.' to report at the vestry of the cathedral, where a fellow-private, a professional organist, was to give a recital.

. . . Arrived at the vestry, I was informed by an N.C.O. that I was to conduct an informal service between the musical items. Needless to say the information staggered me, but, being by now thoroughly imbued with the soldier's lesson of unquestioning obedience, I seized cassock and surplice and some dignitary's M.A. hood and carried on. I gave the Blessing from the High Altar, an act which presumably had not been performed by a humble Curate for some decades. I was informed afterwards that the Dean had entered the Cathedral while this unauthorised Service was going on and was consumed with horrified indignation when informed by a verger that worship was being conducted by a Private in the R.A.M.C.! . . .

On 30 July Thomas, one of the first of his company to volunteer for service at the front, embarked on a troopship at Devonport for an 'unknown destination'. His lengthy description of the voyage, with its crowded discomforts and its routine of parades, lectures and inspections, has very little in common with the convivial—and spiritual—scenes in the officers' quarters depicted in *Tell England*, except for the undercurrent of mounting excitement as to what was in store. Religion is confined to four brief diary entries:

. . . Chat with Chaplain trying to arrange Communion for tomorrow . . . I am Mess Orderly today so cannot attend early service . . . Church Parade at 11 a.m. Chaplain spoke on 'And He shall be a hiding place.' Never saw such a fine setting for a service, or for the singing of the National Anthem. The poop of the ship and well-deck packed solid with khaki—limitless blue seas around us and a flaming sun overhead . . . Attended Communion service in Tea Lounge on Boat Deck. Ten men and one officer—out of nearly 1500. Sermon from 'Banner over him was love' . . .

Thomas reached Gallipoli a month before Raymond, and in time to witness something of the last flare-up of the fighting before the final stalemate set in. It was from Mudros on the island of Lemnos, headquarters of the General Staff, now congested with the wounded and sick, that a destroyer transported his contingent to Suvla Bay, in the northern sector of the Peninsula. The date was 15 August, eight days after 20,000 fresh troops had been landed in the bay in an all-out bid for a breakthrough, and savage fighting, with charges and counter-charges, was still in progress in the rugged hinterland.

. . . We rushed swiftly on towards a bay shaped like a horseshoe glaring yellow in the sun, with low hills rising behind it. At first it seemed entirely bare of life and it was only when we came close in that we could see that it was really swarming with men and mules and carts and stores. Our destroyer cast anchor and horse barges came alongside, into which we were packed, and motor lighters towed us ashore.

I carried with me, besides the thin khaki uniform I had on, a rolled overcoat, water bottle, mess tin, haversack (containing two shirts, eight pairs of socks, six handkerchiefs, one pair of pyjamas, two towels, soap, shaving tackle, notebook and pencil, and prayer book), 'iron rations', my cigarette case (full), pipe and pouch, and two boxes of matches.

We struggled on to the beach and at once were set to work unloading officers' baggage and medical chests. I had just hoisted an officer's valise when a sudden tremendous crash behind me made me drop it. I thought a shell must have exploded but on looking round discovered it was only the firing of a six-inch gun on a cruiser in the bay. That was the first noise of a long series of noises which were to continue day and night for four months . . .

The scene was a beautiful one, the sun shining brilliantly on Suvla Bay and Imbros, whose blue bulk confronted us across the water. Suddenly the heavy roll and crackle of rifle-fire, swelling louder and louder over the saucer-like rim of hill behind us, reminded us of the grim business for which we had come. We fell in—most of us with a feeling of shakiness—but there was no getting out of the boat now, we were fairly launched and committed to the Adventure.

Slowly we moved off in the gathering dusk, through clouds of dust raised by the swarming mule trains and light Indian carts driven by mysterious and much bedraped Sikhs, and began to climb the ridge behind Suvla, using a dry 'nullah'. Then suddenly came the first bullet with a 'fizz' like a monster mosquito and then 'thump' into the side of the gully. More and more flew over as we neared the fighting.

It was very dark now. Suddenly a halt was called and half our men were led off into the darkness while the other half were ordered to remain where we were. Two sergeants and an officer were busy over an indistinct blurr under the gully bank, a 'hand' was needed and I ran up to find that it consisted of three Turks, one dead and two badly wounded. Our first sight of blood and the meaning of War.

After this a connected account of that first night becomes impossible—it is merely the recollection of a disordered nightmare. I remember the tremendous crash of rifle and machine gun fire close to and the 'thump' 'thump' of bullets and sparks flying from the stones while an officer and six of us pushed through the scrub towards the curve of a hill which showed darkly against the night sky. Between the bursts of fire the silence was broken by agonising cries which will always haunt me. Seemingly from all about that hill there were voices crying 'Ambulance', 'Stretcher-bearers', 'Oh damn you my leg's broken' and then again 'Stretcher-bearers'.

It was horrible, we would start for a voice and it would cease and another far away would begin. That hillside was a shambles. Evidently there had been fierce hand-to-hand fighting there a few hours ago, rifles, kits, water-bottles, khaki, Turkish tunics and headgear were strewn everywhere among the scrub. While we were following a phantom-like voice we came suddenly on a half dug trench which an RAMC officer had made into a combined mortuary and first aid station. As we set furiously to work sorting the dead from the living, there reeled among us out of the darkness an officer raving 'My men

have taken that bloody hill but they're dying of thirst.'
He passed on and we continued our ghastly work.

I found myself one of a party of six told off to carry to
the base a man shot through the breast. We linked hands
and shuffled off with no idea of our whereabouts, the
poor fellow we were bearing moaning piteously at every
stumble. The hot night was thick with the whirr of
bullets, the sharp metallic cry of crickets, the ghastly calls
of undiscovered wounded and the sickly smell of Gallipoli thyme. We blundered on, trying to find the rough
path by which we had come but getting more lost at each
step. Now and then we would catch a glimpse of Suvla
Bay with the hospital ship aglow with the lamps of
fairyland, but try as we would we did not seem to get
nearer to them . . .

The detail with which Thomas was able to record his
baptism by fire indicates that, even in nightmare situations,
he kept his nerve, and was able to lay that ghost of being too
'soft' to stand up to it all. During the next few days he was
kept busy as a stretcher-bearer, stumbling with wounded
along the hillside mule-tracks by night, by day under shellfire
(once seeing a man killed and several wounded within yards
of him) and experiencing the agonies of thirst under a
burning sun and the ever-present torment of flies, regarded
by many as the worst hardship of the campaign.

On 21 August Thomas had a fleeting glimpse of what was
to prove the last major action of the campaign. His brief
account is of interest in indicating how much in the dark the
Tommy was as to what was going on, relying on the wildest
of rumours to make sense of the campaign.

In fact this was a final attempt at a breakthrough, and the
'incomparable' 29th Division had been brought round from
the Helles sector in the south to lead an assault on two
dominating hills rising from the Suvla plain. On the after-

noon of 21 August, in stifling heat, unseasonable fog and amid the flames from tinder-dry scrub and gorse set alight by shellfire, the British troops, watched by Sir Ian Hamilton, the Commander-in-Chief, and his staff from a neighbouring height, threw themselves in vain against the Turkish strong-holds. There were 5,000 casualties in what Churchill described as 'this dark battlefield of fog and flame'.

Of all this Thomas was apparently unaware as he watched the preliminary bombardment by the British Fleet:

As a spectacle it was wonderful—though of course mere child's play to the smallest of these affairs in Flanders. The ships were stationed 'en echelon', forming a line of guns from which there belched forth a cloud of smoke lit with yellow flashes. Then would come the crash of the explosion and on the low-lying ground of Anarfat great plumes of earth and stones splashed up in black, white and yellow fountains. The whole district bombarded seemed to be going up like Sodom and Gomorrah in smoke to heaven. Away to the left ships' guns were making wonderful shooting at a line of trenches on the very crest of a hill. Again and again the column-like spout of the explosion would rise from what appeared to be the brown line of the trench itself.

Then, in the westering light of the evening sun, we saw the sheen of bayonets as our men went forward, and in the short intervals between the crashing of the naval guns there came to us the rolling crackle of rifle fire and the stutter of the machine guns. This was all we saw of the attack of August 21st, the last real attempt at a major operation in the campaign, though we should all have been incredulous if we had been told so then . . .

In Thomas's journal of the rest of the campaign up to the evacuation, there is little of what he describes as 'war-like proceedings' or 'the spice of war'. Amounting to some

16,000 words, it is a detailed, and mostly cheerful, account of a stretcher-bearer's life at the front. Its interest, in the context of this book, lies in its occasional allusions to the 'parson' side of the 'parson-private'. And the conclusion seems to be that, while losing no opportunity in joining the faithful in worship, Thomas made little headway with his missionary aim of getting in 'real touch' with men to whom 'the religion of Jesus had ceased to exist'. In his few references to encounters with Tommies not in his immediate circle, sympathy seems to be mixed with something like antipathy.

The exclusive nature of the services in which Thomas participated is indicated in his description of a Communion service held by a Methodist chaplain on Suvla Beach on his first Sunday on the Peninsula:

I went with another parson ranker and a Methodist minister who shared with two others my 'sand-hole'. The service was held in a hollow among the sand-dunes, the 'elements' consisted of pieces of army biscuit on a paten which half an hour earlier had been the bottom of a tobacco tin; the wine was water seasoned with a lemonade cube—the reason for the insertion of the lemonade cube was a mystery to me at the time—perhaps it was intended to make a difference from ordinary water. Anyhow no better substitute could be devised and we received the distribution in faith and were not a little comforted.

In the evening a few of us gathered together and, with the help of two prayer books, managed to sing a few well-known hymns. I gave the Absolution and the Blessing, while the Methodist Chaplain led in extempore prayer. There was no feeling of constraint in either Service: there was need of God to the few of us who believed in Him, forms had ceased to have any meaning to us. We realised our oneness in Christ and that 'where two or three of us were gathered together, there was He in the midst of us.'

Throughout September and October (when he shared a hillside dugout above their hospital camp with a Primitive Methodist minister, a probationary Baptist minister and two others) Thomas conducted regular Sunday services. The Commanding Officer had agreed that he and another parson-ranker in the Corps should be excused Sunday duties as much as possible.

. . . My brother priest had contrived to get hold of Communion vessels and surplice, enclosed in the regulation case, from an army chaplain who had left the Peninsula. This was of course invaluable and gave a fitting method of celebrating the Holy Mystery which otherwise would have had to be performed in the makeshift fashion of the Methodist's celebration on that first Sunday.

There was some difficulty about wine but this was eventually obtained from the Quartermaster at Anzac under the guise of 'medical comforts'. Wafers we obtained from the nearest Roman Catholic chaplain, bread being at that time a thing unknown to us. We took alternative Sundays as celebrant and server, the server at the morning Communion giving the address at the evening Service.

For many weeks the Communion service was held in the open by the Corps flagstaff, wherein many bullets had embedded themselves. Our altar was made of empty boxes and the congregation knelt upon the ground. How vividly the words of the later Trinity Collects will always recall those simple Masses: 'Keep us by Thy help from all things hurtful', 'O God our refuge and strength', 'that we may be ready both in body and soul.' Some eight or ten of us would be gathered there in the cold clear morning air at six o'clock before the sun came over the top of Sari Bair. Sometimes a dozen would come together, and once we reached sixteen with the help of some New Zealanders from a Battery close by.

The evening Services were subject to considerable change in time, as the exigencies of War demanded, but we always managed to get in a service of some kind before set of sun. Nothing could have been much further from the ideal of a Solemn Evensong than those Services of ours. To begin with our method of summoning our parishioners was one to which a missionary to the Sandwich Islands would hardly be reduced. We borrowed the cook-house gong—an empty shell case—upon which we battered furiously with the long spoon used for stirring the bully-beef stew.

When we gathered a sufficient number to warrant a start being made, we divided our flock into groups of four or five, who did their best to get a glimpse of the tattered hymnbook which was all we could allow to each group. Hymns not infrequently came to grief through the mistake of key at the outset: the first line would go all right and then often enough we would find ourselves reaching up to notes rarely touched by prima donnas in their prime, or scraping down to depths untouched by Santley!

The sermon was nearly always dogged by misfortune. Generally, as soon as one had given out one's text (the time being that of the 'evening hate'), 'whoosh' 'whoosh' would sound above us and then 'crump' 'crash' on the sand-dunes by the sea, and half your congregation would turn round to see the column of black or yellow smoke spout up fountain-like from the ground. Worse was to follow. We had five 60-pounders down there and almost immediately after the explosion of the Turkish shells there would shoot out five wicked looking tongues of flame and the splitting crashes following on the voice of someone in the battery giving the number of the gun as it was 'eased off'.

And yet in old days we had heard of clergy being annoyed and put off by some old lady coughing in the body of the church! To have stopped speaking on account of noise in Gallipoli would have been to condemn oneself to perpetual silence. Guns or no guns the service would go on and often the last lingering touch of rose on the peaks of Imbros would fade away as one gave the Blessing of 'the peace of God which passeth all understanding' . . .

While in this camp Thomas's status as a kind of honorary padre was further recognised by his Commanding Officer when he detailed him to conduct burial services in the camp cemetery.

. . . When we first arrived the Cemetery contained some twenty of the heroic dead and had very considerably increased by the time we left. There were always two open graves waiting to receive the bodies of those about to die. Often I was taken from my ordinary duties to bury some poor fellow who had been brought down from the trenches and had died on the way.

There was something unutterably pathetic in those simple burials, the body being laid on a stretcher, blood soaking through from the mortal wound, the dead boy still wearing his soiled and tattered khaki in which he had fought and toiled and eaten and slept and now slept the last long sleep. How smart and soldierly he must have looked at his last home parade with sun-helmet and puggaree; almost certainly a photograph of at least his Company in their overseas kit stood on some mantelpiece in England. And now—the wreck of what once was a man, thin and wasted with exhaustion, mangled, smashed beyond recognition, with battered misshapen helmet resting over crossed hands on his breast.

At that very moment some fond mother or wife or sweetheart in all probability was telling her friends how my Tom had gone to Gallipoli. But at least these received orderly Christian burial, with the great words of Eternal Hope read over them. Hundreds lay rotting in the burning sun where they had fallen in the cruel scrub of No Man's Land . . .

Thomas's sympathy and concern for the Tommy are not in doubt. But that he had by now abandoned any hopes of his service in the ranks proving a 'missionary enterprise without parallel' is apparent by an allusion in this part of the journal to an unexpected offer that was made to him. His reactions make it clear that he would have had little hesitation in exchanging his role as 'parson-private' for that of fully-fledged padre (a move that would have taken him in one step from lowly private to the substantive rank of captain).

. . . At about this time the other parson-private and myself were summoned to Divisional Headquarters. Our consciences revealing nothing of which we were ashamed, we presented ourselves before the august body of 'brass hats' without a tremor. We were ushered into a dugout of such dimensions and comforts as we had not dreamed of as being possible and were asked if we would care to have our names put forward for the position of Acting Chaplains as it had come to the knowledge of the Olympians that we were in Orders and as it was acknowledged that there was a great dearth of chaplains at the time.

Needless to say we were quite willing to fall in with the proposition and we were informed that the application would follow the usual channels and in due course we would hear more of the matter. Some six weeks afterwards we were summoned before our Commanding Officer who informed us that the proposition had not received favourable recognition from the Home Authorities, who preferred to send Chaplains straight from England—so we were bidden to 'carry on' in our present capacity.

I remember it was a great disappointment at the time, but the disappointment soon wore off—we were too busy to bother our heads about it. Still it has always seemed to me rather a silly piece of red-tapism as we were salted to the game and climate and probably more fit for the job than a fresh and juicy curate straight from the Old Country would be! . . .

Thomas mentions only two encounters with padres in his sector. One was a Roman Catholic padre, who invited him to share his 'superior dugout' in the officers' lines:

Needless to say I was agreeable to this and for a week or so we lived together. He was a bluff and hearty Irishman and a most cheery person to meet, though like most Roman Catholic priests of my acquaintance very loath to talk about the question of Unity. In spite of many efforts to draw him on I could never get beyond the merest fringe of the subject. He read his Office regularly while I had recourse to my well-thumbed and tattered Prayer Book.

Though conversation on Religious topics languished he was full of anecdotes on men and matters generally and was one of the most efficient 'fly-strafers' I have ever met. Before we settled down for the night he insisted on my doing my part in half an hour's strenuous 'swatting' of these noxious pests. However the roof of the dugout was always black with them within a few minutes of the cessation of hostilities, so the nightly strafe did not seem to be worth the energy expended . . .

The other padre was encountered in the camp Thomas's unit was moved to in November, a large rest camp on the beach two miles away, the camp to which they had all this time been carrying the wounded and sick prior to embarkation on the hospital ship. From Thomas's description it is evident that this was the kind of padre he aspired to be:

Very shortly after our arrival a 'pukka' Church of England padre joined us. He was young, energetic and merry-eyed, altogether just the person, or parson, for the job. He was always welcome in the tents and rarely left without cheering up the individual or the group with whom he had been talking. He exuded an atmosphere of genuine cheeriness which was far removed from that most depressing cloak of insinuative and assumed jocularity which is donned by a certain type of Divine.

If he found a squad of men securing tent ropes or filling sandbags he was always ready to turn to and lend a hand in the most natural manner possible. He kept a 'baccy' which agreed with me and often he would call me in to his superior dugout for a yarn on things in general. He allowed me to Celebrate the Eucharist on alternate Sundays and act as his 'lector' at the crowded lantern-lit evening Services in the swaying wind-rocked E.P. tents. I have often wondered what became of him. The impression he left was of the best—and 'so said all of us' . . .

What impression Thomas left on his fellow-Tommies can only be guessed at. That the impression left on him by the majority of Tommies was very far from being that of the 'lovable creatures' lauded by Padre Monty can be gauged from two extracts. The first relates to the early days in his first camp when he was switched from stretcher-bearing duties to construction work in the improvement of the camp.

. . . As one of a 'gang' told off for such labours I gained some insight into the workings of the mind common to the people who do these tasks. They have no idea of, or respect for, the brain which directs, but merely envy that one man should be so fortunate as to have nothing more laborious to perform than the ordering of other people to work. The old and oft-repeated growse we had grown familiar with at home, namely that we had not joined the Army to do this and that menial task but to fight the enemy or succour the wounded, was repeated again at the front, where it ought to have been obvious that our labours were quite necessary and even vital for the work we had come to do. However, 'growling' is the perquisite of the 'under dog' and perhaps, as only a temporary member of the 'unter-canine' fraternity, I ought not to have resented their attitude. After all they and their ancestors have 'humped' the heavy work of the world for centuries . . .

A more sweeping categorisation comes towards the end of the journal, when Thomas was serving as a nursing orderly at the beach-head camp in hospital tents dealing with a constant stream of sick and emaciated men, most of them suffering from dysentery.

. . . In the early afternoon the patients would be turned out to sun themselves on the beach near to which the tents were ranged, the weather now being mercifully fine. You would see crowds of soldiers sitting on the beach in all states of undress, employed in the universal Gallipoli pursuit of 'doing in' at least some of the loathsome animalculae which made life such a burden to us all.

Then back everyone would come into the tents, tea was fetched and distributed amid grumblings and growlings as of half-starved wolves, the 'fag' would be produced and the sickeningly familiar 'Gi' us a light, mate,'

would re-echo on every hand. For the most part conversation centred round one or other of two subjects,
'Beer' and 'Women', the two things without which life
would not be worth living for the people who have never
had the education or opportunity to cherish any other
ideals.

Here and there one would come across the refined face
of a lad of the Public School type bent over some
well-thumbed copy of a pocket Kipling or a Golden
Treasury, carefully preserved through Heaven knows
what ups and downs of the fighting line. These were in
my experience invariably more cheerful in adversity, less
selfish and less querulous than their brethren of coarser
mould, though possibly the 'grousing' of the latter was
more habit than anything else. But generally speaking
the 'pest-houses' of Gallipoli were full of cursing and
bitterness . . .

It was only among the more educated Tommies in his
immediate circle (including the Primitive Methodist and
Baptist ministers who shared his first dugout) that Thomas
appears to have made any close contact so far as spiritual
matters were concerned. There is a nostalgic reference to
heart-to-heart talks with his fellow-stretcher-bearers as they
trudged back the two miles from Suvla beach after conducting to the rest camp yet another batch of 'the broken and the
sick—dirty, lousy, with hollow cheeks and sunken eyes,
tattered clothes and abandoned aspect, the human wreckage
of the campaign.'

. . . How clearly those night returns to camp come back
to me. Twinkling in the far distance our camp light
would shine out across the scrub, and far out on the
Anzac slopes of Sari Bair we could see the signal lamp
which showed the foremost of our trenches. Often an
action of attack or defence would flicker up on the circle

of hills which bounded our position and a fine sight it was to see the Verey lights, red, white and blue, flare up into the sky, the slow dropping white stars and the rolling volume of musketry and the vicious 'phat' and 'phizz' of 'overs' and 'spents' which passed us or struck sparks from the stones at our feet.

It was on occasions like this that one's companion or companions would open out and many a time I have listened to tales of things 'done and ill-done' in the days before the war; of attempts made again and again to get on the right track, of the power of a man's 'mates' to drag him down; of the organised opposition to Good in workshop and yards, the crushing weight of sheer numbers on the side of the enemy; of the tiny rushlight of Christianity in the wilderness of London represented by a mission church or local Bethel. Again one heard of the home troubles, the heroic attempts of a family to keep Father or Mother from 'the Drink', and rarely, as a pleasant relief, the tale of a lad who had found happiness in the Catholic Church as a 'server' and of his devotion to Father So-and-so and his joy in taking part with him in the Service of Christ . . .

It is here that Thomas comes remarkably close to Padre Monty in an assessment of the most effective form of Anglican worship at the front. Monty's pronouncement, backed by personal conviction, had come in one of his homilies to Ray and Doe:

. . . The outstanding fact of my experience has been the astonishing loyalty to his chaplain and his church of that awful phenomenon, the young High Church fop, the ecclesiastical youth. He has known what his chaplains are for, and what they can give him; he hasn't needed to be looked up and persuaded to do his religious duties, but has rather looked up his chaplain and persuaded him to do them. He has got up early and walked a mile to Mass. His faith, for all its foppery, has stood four-square . . .

Thomas, a Broad Churchman, comes with seeming reluctance to the same conclusion:

. . . I here set it on record, without prejudice, that the few to whom Religion was anything more than a name were definitely High Churchmen and the centre of their Faith was the Sacrament of Mass, as they preferred to call it. They took a definite stand on definite teaching. The ordinary ex-Sunday School scholar and ex-choirman —the great mass of Broad or Low Church production —were as 'reeds shaken in the wind' or 'houses built on sand', without strength or stability. This I mention merely as a fact which came so strikingly to my notice that the suppression of it would be to misrepresent deliberately actual experience . . .

The last, and most memorable, service at which Thomas officiated was on 28 November, Advent Sunday and his own 33rd birthday. It was two weeks before the evacuation, at a time when the fighting had been temporarily abandoned. Two days before the heavens had opened, and God could be said to be on neither side as a deluge of rain, lashed by howling winds, flooded the opposing trenches and formed mountain torrents down which a gruesome cargo was swept to the beaches.

. . . The foreshore was strewn with odd-shaped humps and heaps of what looked like meat and proved to be the remnants of human bodies. Some were complete, others so mutilated as to show only the trunk. Odd limbs were also to be seen at intervals along the shore. All that I saw were Turks. Most of them were naked, though the sodden rags of uniform still clung to the remains of some. They were of good physique. One magnificently shaped man I noticed particularly. He had been shot through the throat and both his arms were stretched above his head in a life-like attitude.

Some bodies bore traces of having been painted green, and of one body enough remained to make clear that women had taken some part in the fighting line. The bodies were in all stages of preservation and corruption and were a gruesome sight after the grim night we had passed. I was one of those told off for the burying of these mutilated fragments of humanity—an unsavoury task for which we received a special reward of a packet of ten Woodbine apiece . . .

The storm was followed by a three-day snow blizzard, during which men froze to death in the trenches. Conditions all around were of 'unutterable wretchedness' on the day Thomas celebrated his birthday and, at the morning service, found that his own faith had (in Monty's words) 'stood four-square'.

. . . The blizzard was getting well into its stride as I made my way to the tent where we held our Communion Service. It was my turn to act as Celebrant and I am not likely ever to forget that Service. The Chaplain and I set up our Altar, both of us blue with cold, with dirty swollen hands and beards of three days' growth. Three heroic souls turned up and I gave them the Bread and Wine of Life, strangely vested as I was in a muddied overcoat with a battered ear-flapped Army cap upon my head. It was a memorable Service in more ways than one. The silence was so intense and as unfamiliar as the cold—indeed no sound of gun or rifle broke the silence of those snow-bound days. And further the power of the familiar words was so great as to render me at any rate unconscious of the unhappy conditions which surrounded us . . .

Thomas was in as wretched a condition physically as most of the sick crowding the hospital tents when the time came at last to vacate the peninsula. Added to mild dysentery, he had contracted dropsy. Day by day his legs grew heavier and more swollen until 'the knee joint had entirely disappeared and I staggered about on two supports that looked like blown out sausages.' On 13 December the order came to embark for Mudros, and Thomas gritted his teeth:

> . . . I had made up my mind I would not be 'carried' as long as I could stand up. I had to fix my attention on some group of stones on the beach a hundred yards or so ahead and *will* my disgusting legs to get me there. At one point an open space of ground was being sniped intermittently at extreme rifle range. I set off in my swaying shambling walk and my erratic course must have disconcerted the sniper as, though he had a longer time than usual, he got nowhere near me. At last the beginning of the pier was in sight, with a 'lighter' alongside. I remember my intense anxiety lest it should be filled before my turn came. But no, my luck was in and I obtained a place . . .

The parson-private had proved, if nothing else, the strength and stability of his own faith. But, as he looked back at the beach where he had landed with such high hopes four months before, there could have been no real sense of a mission achieved. His 'tiny rushlight of Christianity' had done little more than flicker amid the prevailing Godlessness.

> . . . The night was cold and heavy clouds were drifting over the moon. An hour dragged itself away—should we never move off? Joy! at last the engine had started and we were under weigh, pushing out into the darkness while the familiar sounds of the night came to our ears—the snap of rifle shots, the occasional mutter of a machine gun, the cry of the crickets.

Now we were really away and our feelings of thankfulness might have free play! Yet curiously enough we were very silent. Like all places where one had really lived the old Peninsula made its impression felt. We were leaving behind us an experience which would make an indelible impression upon all our minds. But above all it was the thought that we were leaving without having really accomplished anything that held us silent and more than a little sad . . .

Some 25 years later, a vicar at Haywards Heath in Sussex, Thomas was able to exchange reminiscences of those traumatic times with a near neighbour who had served at Gallipoli at the same time, though in a different sector —Ernest Raymond. And it was more than the 'Great Adventure' that the two had in common. For the parson-private had gone on to become a 'pukka padre'. After recovering his health (and marrying his fiancée) early in 1916, Thomas had been an acting chaplain in the Royal Navy. After two relatively uneventful years ministering to the crews of cruisers he was transferred to the RAF, where he served as chaplain until 1920.

Mark Thomas, born in 1918, who works with an underwriting syndicate at Lloyd's, recalls seeing his father and Raymond deep in conversation, though he does not know what they talked about or whether they could find any common ground with reference to their missions as padres, now that Raymond had renounced his faith. He remembers Raymond as a 'literary' man and going to Christmas parties at his home where the games were apt to be a bit daunting —like picking a 'subject' out of a hat and having to make an extempore speech on it.

Thomas has no doubt that his father's Gallipoli experiences, which he often recalled, had a profound effect on him. 'Switching from the quiet life of a curate in a country parish to roughing it as a Tommy at the front had a great leavening effect' he says. 'It made him realise what the average working man had to put up with. Though his parishes were never in working class areas—Melksham, Wiltshire, St. Minver and St. Enodoc in Cornwall (where he became friendly with John Betjeman), Bexhill, Haywards Heath and Hove—he always kept close contact with his poorer parishioners, churchgoers or not, and played an active role in British Legion Clubs.'

Thomas, who died in 1960 aged 77, paid no return visit to the scenes of his brief but unforgettable adventures as a parson-private. Raymond did so, shortly after the war while still a padre, clambering up to those heights overlooking the Dardanelles which the British troops had never succeeded in reaching. He did not look for the 'Tell England' inscription mentioned in his novel because it did not exist. It, and the title to his best-seller, had been inspired by an epitaph dating back to pagan times. Ascribed to the Spartan Simonides after the battle of Thermopylae, its stark brevity, invoking no gods, pared of heroics, moved Ruskin to describe it as 'the noblest group of words ever uttered by man': 'Tell the Spartans, stranger, that here we lie, obedient to their laws.'

Memorials abound on the Gallipoli Peninsula, but they are all to the Allied dead. With none of the Christians' preoccupation with death, the Turks buried their dead in anonymous communal graves. There are now few veterans left to make the pilgrimage to the old battlefields, still criss-crossed with crumbling trenches. Peasants ploughing their fields occasionally unearth a rusted bullet or fragment of a shell. Turkish gardeners, under the auspices of the Allied War Graves Commission, tend the cemeteries, mostly sited on the heights around which the bloodiest battles were fought.

'Obedient to their laws', here on this rarely visited peninsula lie the dead of both sides, victims of a campaign in which few could have confidently avowed that God or Allah had the ascendancy. In the Allied cemeteries, indeed, there are not even the customary crosses to hint at a crusade. That apart, Raymond's *alter ego*, Padre Monty, must have warmly approved the description of the scene by Alan Moorehead, in his classic *Gallipoli* (published in 1956), which strangely echoes his musings on the levelling hand of death.

. . . Each cemetery is surrounded by a bank of pines, and the graves themselves, which are not marked by crosses but by marble plaques in the ground, are thickly planted with cypresses and junipers, arbutus and rosemary and such flowering shrubs as the Judas tree. In winter moss and grass cover the ground, and in summer a thick carpet of pine needles deadens the footfall. There is no sound except for the wind in the trees and the calls of the migrating birds who have found these places the safest sanctuary on the peninsula. The effect upon the visitor's mind is not that of the tragedy of death but of an immense tranquillity, of the continuity of things.

CHAPTER FOUR

PARSON AT PASSCHENDAELE

AFTER LUNCH SAT with the doctor in the mess. He says
the men and officers think a lot of my going up the
line but I do not see why they should. They have to, so
why shouldn't I?

So wrote the Rev Maurice Murray, a middle-aged country parson turned padre, shortly after the bloodiest battle in
history had foundered in the Flanders mud in the winter of
1917. At the age of 47 he had shared many of the hazards of
the units he served in the crater-pocked morass of the Ypres
Salient. But from his own phlegmatic account it is difficult to
gauge how much he felt he had achieved in the service of
God.

'My experiences compared with those of the humblest
fighting man are not worth recording', he writes at the end of
the 70,000-word copy he made from the pocket diaries in
which he had made daily entries throughout his year in
France. 'Yet I have put them down here in the hopes that
some day my children, and possibly their children, may care
to read them.'

Educated at Lancing College and Queen's College, Oxford, ordained in 1896, Murray was the son of a clergyman
and came from a long line of clergy. Two of his forbears had
been bishops. Two of his brothers had opted like him for the

Church. And to him the Anglican rituals and traditions in which he was so deeply rooted had as much validity on the battlefield as in a country parish.

As Rector of Leybourne, a small parish near West Malling in Kent, married with two young daughters, Murray began badgering his bishop to be sent to the front early in 1915, only to be told he was too old. In 1916 he was appointed Chaplain to the troops in nearby Leybourne Park Camp, but still hankered to be where the action was and continued to badger. 'Even when I had finally obtained my Bishop's permission', he writes, 'the Chaplain General tried hard to dissuade me from service in France, the "real front", as he said, being at home.'

In the event Murray, a keen sportsman, proved no liability so far as physique and stamina were concerned. At the base hospital near Rouen where he spent the first four months (and where he records taking part in football matches, even boxing bouts), he was soon complaining that the life was 'far too comfortable'. Transferred to the Ypres sector he showed that he could keep up with the youngest Tommy, whether on the march or in the line. Invalided home (to his chagrin) with a burst eardrum near the start of the Third Battle of Ypres, he had no hesitation in returning to the front. 'It seemed quite homey to be up in the front line once more' reads one entry.

From the pages of his diary Murray emerges as a likeable man, modest, courageous, conscientious. What is missing is any spiritual content. Regular services and celebrations of Holy Communion (usually to only a handful of men), sermons with such titles as 'Jacob's Ladder', 'Cleaning of the Temple' and 'Going to Jerusalem', ministrations to the dying, burial services, are meticulously recorded, but with less comment than he attaches to camp concerts and sporting events.

For Murray there appears to have been something a little

suspect about an other than formal approach to religion. Of one Tommy he met he writes that he was 'rather religious in a rather nauseating way'. Of an evangelical service in a dugout near the front line he writes:

> I walked down the duckboards to the 'church' where were notices of nonconformist and Church of England services all fitted in rather well so as not to clash. It is a nice little dugout and at the time of my visit full of nonconformist soldiers with whom an earnest Welsh padre was praying in English. He was thin and tall and wore no robes. He had that earnest Revivalist look and his voice was at once melodious and odious.

As a young curate Murray's parishes had included St Paul's, Walworth, then one of the toughest districts in south-east London. He was no stranger to the working classes, in town and country. It is the more surprising that the diary reveals so little sense of personal identification with the men he served. Though he frequently risked his life in visits to the trenches (usually with gifts of cigarettes) and assisting in first aid posts, the Tommies remain anonymous, shadowy figures.

Only once does Murray record anything like a heart-to-heart encounter with a named Tommy. It took place in a pill-box, while the guns were blazing around Passchendaele, and one cannot imagine that the Tommy concerned gained much sustenance or enlightenment from it.

> Had a nice talk with Pronger about 'God stopping the war' and 'allowing the war'—two 'stock' yet most natural difficulties to be met with and seriously faced when talking to the men. I told Pronger what I believed. That, though of man's making, much good has and will come out of the war—sacrifice, love, opportunities for women, love of home after the war, usefulness and

handiness in the home, love of land and agriculture, self-denial especially after the war to pay for it all, and lastly immunity from future warfare. I often think that these men (I don't know exactly what Pronger is at home but he is, I suppose, one of the 'working class') speak very nicely and reverently about God, more reverently than we clergy often do.

Murray's avowed aim as a padre was service to others ('to be of *use* by God's help'). Church services and ministrations to the dying apart, he appears to have equated this more with the physical and material welfare of the men than with spiritual and moral guidance. Only on one occasion— shortly after his arrival in France—does he betray any misgivings about the task he has set himself, and, indeed, about the strength of his own faith.

He had spent that day, 22 January 1917, touring the wards of No. 8 General Hospital, just outside Rouen, meeting the medical staff and the officers of his mess, viewing the chapel he was to share with his Presbyterian and Roman Catholic opposite numbers ('dirty and cold, and the man in charge, a Scotchman, incompetent'). His long entry ends:

I frankly do not like things here so far. The atmosphere strikes me as absolutely irreligious and the language is not particularly good either, but I do not intend to be downhearted. Must use tact and try and win everybody and try to be of *use* by God's help. I fear especially for my own spiritual life. I must pray more. I have never felt the need and help of religion more somehow than tonight.

Murray's working hours during his four months at Rouen were mostly devoted to regular services, visits to the sick and wounded in the hospital (with accommodation for 1,200 'fluctuating according to the fighting') and the censoring and writing of letters. These are typical diary entries:

. . . I conducted parties of walking wounded to various wards and gave out cigarettes on arrival. Also acted as stretcher-bearer which I found stretches one's arms out well. I have never seen anything like the mud on the men. You could not possibly tell who or what they were, officers and men all looked alike, unshaven, hollow-eyed and covered with mud and blood . . .

. . . A man called Best in D3 is very ill, also Erickson. The former is dying, they think. The latter fights well. I prayed with Best. He was having oxygen just before I got to the ward and was wandering, poor fellow. Still, God and the men in the ward could hear and the latter joined in the prayers . . .

. . . I committed to the ground 13 poor bodies from the troop train accident, using the words of the Committal individually, and making the sign of the Cross over each grave. Then I collected the empty cartridges from the volley firing to send them to the relatives at home as some tangible memento . . .

After breakfast I went to Rouen to the padre meeting with Bishop Gwynne. There were 20 Church of England padres present. The Bishop spoke to us of how at the beginning of the war Generals etc. were in the habit of complaining of padres being up in the trenches. Now they complained if they were not . . .

. . . I have given up smoking, pudding and all meat this Lent and only hope that it may be a means of subduing the flesh. I have got too fat lately. We all have a great deal of food, far too much and too good . . .

. . . Visited D3 and was with poor Goddard when he died. I committed his brave and patient soul to God. Sister Macmillan cried bitterly as she loves all her 'boys'. Goddard's father and mother are on the way here and he had asked Sister Macmillan and the orderly to come to his wedding when he got to England. All his sweetheart's

letters came back today, having gone astray somehow . . .

. . . I talked to a Tank Officer—he calls his tank
'Peggy' after his wife. Another is called Charlie Chaplin,
another 'The Iron Devil'. I think Peggy sounds nice . . .

. . . Went to Rouen and saw the A.C.G. I told him that
the whole life here was far too comfortable and that I
should continue to worry him until I went up the line . . .
In the evening I boxed with Hepple on the badminton
court and I got him on the nose but he hit me about and
got my wind but I enjoyed the bout. Hepple is a very
good boxer and very quick indeed and a hard hitter . . .

. . . About 10.30 p.m. I was sent for by Cobcroft of
A1 who was dying. I prayed with him and asked him if he
would like to receive the Sacrament. He said 'yes' most
earnestly and wistfully so I ran to the mess, got my
Communion things and two candles (as there is no light
in the Chapel) and there I simply consecrated the Elements, receiving them myself and then taking them to
him. I cannot see what else I could have done and
necessity knows no law. I think I will write to my dear
Bishop Harmer about this and my work generally . . .

Thursday May 17 (Ascension Day). I go up to the line
at last! Up at 5.30. Took Celebration with Robinson (the
new padre who succeeds me). There were only five
nurses and ourselves in the Chapel . . . Got trench helmet, THREE gas apparati, first aid things for wounds
(my future wounds!), brassards etc . . .

Murray's destination was the headquarters of the 116th
Brigade of the 39th Division at the village of Wormhoudt in
the Ypres sector. His lengthy description of the three days'
train journey to the front, mostly written en route, is in some
ways the most revealing section of his diary. One glimpses
the man behind the uniform. Here is a country parson, lonely

[121]

and thinking of home as he gazes from his first-class compartment at a tranquil countryside untouched by war, nerving himself for what is to come at the end of the line, there where the action is.

. . . The sun came out very hot at 5.30 p.m. Began to wonder when I should hear the guns. I should have liked to do this journey with someone, an officer or officers, who know about things, but the train seems full of French officers and civilians. Everything is quite quiet all down the train whenever we stop, which is fairly frequently. The distant spires of Rouen looked very beautiful in the heat haze before we turned up the valley. The waits are very long. I can hear the birds singing loudly in the trees by the railway . . .

We stopped a long time at a little station where I saw chalked up on a water hydrant 'Pas d'eau a Buchy'. It began to feel and to look like one of those evenings at Stone when the cowslips were just over and the cherry blossom was all down on the gravel. Also one thought of the Freshers' Match at Oxford and of those wonderful striped flannel suits of the '90's . . .

I must remember these sights for Joan [his eldest daughter]. A man, his wife and two little bare-legged children reunited at a station and many smart country girls pumping up their bicycles after getting out of the train to go to distant farms. It was rather like Firsley. The tops of the orchards looked like hastily mixed pink and white cream. A lot of apple trees are only just in bud, I suppose later sorts . . .

No. 8 General almost seems like home to me now. I began to read but saw some hares in a young wheatfield. The gold of the hares touched by a low-lying sun showed up very much against the vivid green. I wonder when I shall see the first sign of any sort of destruction and the path of past fighting . . .

It is now 7.30. They will be playing badminton at No. 8 and going in to dinner soon. I envy them in a way but would hate myself if I had not persevered in trying to come. French soldiers singing at the upper end of the train . . .

Via Amiens, Calais and Poperinghe, it was not until two nights later that Murray had reached his destination and was able to write: 'Saw star shells, or Very lights, going up at the front line miles away. Heavy guns shook windows most of the night but it appears that this is nothing. I thought that at least the Germans had broken through or that we had smashed out way to Berlin. But no, that was nothing . . .'

During the next seven months that distant front line was to become a familiar part of his 'parish' and he was to see as much as many combatants of the horrors of trench warfare. Despite initial misgivings, he appears to have taken it all in his stride. At one stage he writes, apropos of a letter from an elder brother:

Auriol repeats ad nauseam 'No Murray ever funked yet, thank God', which I cannot help regarding as a somewhat negative virtue on the part of the clan. I don't suppose anyone out here likes shells or any other kind of stuff, heavy or otherwise. Everyone must funk in a sense, I am sure I do often. The only thing is not to show it as it is infectious and bad for morale. That's about all there is to it . . .

That Murray may have had to keep a tighter rein on himself than his diary indicates is suggested by an entry on the second day of his arrival at Brigade headquarters. The only dream recorded, it might even suggest that a subconscious desire to prove his own manhood had been a prime motivation for his repeated requests to be sent to the front.

No guns tonight and slept well. Dreamed that I and another man were arrested and sentenced to be burned alive. An officer took us both over to see the place where we were to die and tried to allay our fears by saying 'You need not worry about the pain as your heads will be screwed into these iron clutches so as to hold your heads in the hottest part, and to get it over quickly'. The odd thing was that we both agreed that it was a most kind thing to have thought of and that no one could object to being burnt under such humane conditions!

Murray's 'parish' comprised four units of the Brigade, the 12th and 13th Sussex, the trench mortar battery and the machine gun company. Ten days after his arrival he marched 17 miles towards the line, for a stretch of 4 miles carrying a sergeant's pack and rifle (weighing 100 lbs), 'to know what it felt like'. His first visit to the front line, on 4 June, was uneventful:

A very hot day indeed. Went up to front firing line with Piper [his orderly]. Very interesting. Our trench was called Threadneedle Street. The plan and idea of the trenches was perfectly wonderful. The men looked very bored and sleepy except those watching and sniping. I wonder what it is all like up here in the dark with star shells going up and men creeping about in No Man's Land wire staking or wire cutting and at listening posts. I took the men some cigarettes and talked with them. They were all full of jokes. We are quite close to the Bosche here. At Turco Farm I believe we are only 40 yards away . . .

Murray's first service in a dugout 'chapel', two miles behind the firing line, was typical of many to come:

I felt so queer to have to go to church in a tin hat and a gas helmet—I had mine at the ready leaning on the right of the little rickety altar. I used ration bread instead of wafers, my stock of which was exhausted, and I had some Brigade headquarters' port wine in my silver flask. I do not think that we padres ought to be burdened with the heavy and unwieldy Holy Communion sets which the Chaplain General gives us in Albemarle Street when we first sally forth . . .

(3 men attended the 7.30 a.m. service, none came at 9.30, 22 at 11, of whom 10 stayed for Holy Communion.)

On 23 July Murray bicycled from Brigade HQ to Poperinghe for a momentous conclave. On the eve of the Third Battle of Ypres, the Archbishop of York had come to give his blessing and encouragement to the padres who would be participating. The service was held in Talbot House, the famous 'Everyman's Club' from which later emanated that 'brotherhood of the trenches', the Toc H movement.

The Archbishop celebrated Holy Communion and gave an address on the words 'The hour is come. Glorify (vindicate) Me that I may vindicate them.' 110 communicants, all padres of 5th Army and 'allied trades', such as Church Army and YMCA. Intercessions taken (inaudibly) by the Archbishop. Conference at 2 p.m. The Archbishop asked several questions but we all got rather discursive, including the Archbishop himself. Still, it was all very friendly and nice and did us good to meet and compare notes.

Our divisional padres met at Cyril's restaurant for tea and Crawley sketched out the arrangements and where we were all to be in the advance, or 'the push'. Crawley drew a plan showing us our jobs. I am to be in an R.A.P. in the front line so feel a bit honoured . . .

Next day Murray went to see the Brigadier. 'I thought he

would be glad to hear that the 13th Sussex had asked for a special service but he dropped a brick by washing out my open air service on the plea that the Battalion might get shelled.' Later he went to see a model of what was to be the field of battle in his sector.

It was a huge model of the same area covered by my map, all done to scale by the Royal Engineers and with a staging round it from which a whole company could be lectured at a time. The children at home would have loved to have seen the trenches and farms and cottages and water all done in miniature.

The Third Battle of Ypres consisted of a series of major actions between 31 July and 30 November. By the time it ended, with the capture of the ruins of Passchendaele but without having achieved a final breakthrough, British losses were estimated at 240,000 (the German total about the same). Murray's account of the opening stages starts on the afternoon of 30 July:

Piper and I went up to Hall Street at 4 p.m. via Garden Trench. Trenches much damaged and almost empty. Found the aid post to which Crawley said that I was to be attached in the charge jointly of two Medical Officers, Anderson and Gatchell. I found them in a baby elephant (small dugout) with a large shed nearby for dressing the wounded. Gatchell and Anderson quarrelled a good deal, beginning by chaffing and ending in real anger, kicking and mud throwing, some of which hit me!
    Heavy shelling all night on both sides. Bullets kept coming 'phitt' into the mud just outside our elephant and a sniper must have had a fixed rifle trained on the left side of it but you could miss it by ducking. I wandered along the trench, or remains of the trench, and got to a deep gallery with about 50 steps down to it. I was minded to

stay there until we went over in the morning, but decided not as the smell was awful before I had descended 10 steps. It was packed with men and they were all down the 'banisters' and on the steps too. I don't think I slept much but can't remember.

31 July. At an early hour our men who were behind us went over. The waves passed over and round us. The advance took place after a tremendous drum fire on our part. Soon after this Lts. Dobbie, Taylor (hit in the eye), Symington and others and 30 Boche came in wounded. Altogether we dressed 530 at this aid post. The Boche were very good as stretcher bearers. I complained about an R.A.M.C. man taking a Boche's gold watch and got given a Boche button as a reward!

The Boche were mostly 255th German Infantry Regt. and some talked English as well as we could. Some of them were very young and one I prayed with as he was dying. I buried two of our boys near the aid post. One was killed by a shell after he had been dressed for slight wounds and had only gone a few yards when a shell got him. The other died on his stretcher.

Piper and I went out and tried to collect wounded. We found one man pretty bad in our trench and got him along after a rather strenuous journey. We ought to have got him over the top of the trench to start with and then to have made across the open but we kept on and could not have got out if we had tried. The mud and loose duck boards made it frightfully difficult. In the end we got him to the aid post. We had been told of another man who had been seen up towards Garden Trench and we found the blood trail but never got him as he had evidently crawled out of the trench and been seen and evacuated.

Our RAP was now getting too far behind the battle to be of as much use as it might so we all moved early in the afternoon to Calf Support Trench and got busy again.

Poor old Piper was hit at 3 p.m. A liaison officer told me where he was. He had taken shelter from the shelling with some others under the lee of a low roofed shed which the Germans had erected, Calf Support being of course one of their trenches. I told Gatchell and he did him up as soon as I had found him. He used the pointed stick which I had given Piper at Poperinghe as a splint and I kicked away a piece of the trench for another.

I sat with him in a dip at the side of the shed, which was 12th Battn. H.Q., till 8 p.m. when at last stretcher bearers came for him. He asked me to sing hymns, 'Abide with me' and 'Sun of my soul'. He had lost a lot of blood before I found him and was very white. His foot was nearly blown off and he was in great pain. I put his head on my knees. We had nothing to eat but I had some water then. Later on we had no water. It rained very hard but the tin roofing kept this and shrapnel off.

Piper had been hit a little further up the dip in the open. I moved the body of the boy who was killed near him as it got so on his nerves being only 2 yards away. The boy's head was pinched between two pieces of rivetting tim- bers and he must have been killed instantly. He lay with his hands up in the air and a red handkerchief in one of them.

We all slept that night in a dugout not far from the 12th B.H.Q. and it rained all night and the dugout, being entered down a slope, filled with water. We had no food. I went out once—the shells were still thick and it was a weird and desolate scene as shown by the star shells.

Before it got dark our Brigade Staff Captain, Tatham, came in to ask the way to where the 13th Sussex and 14th Hants were, up in front of St. Julien at Canopers Trench. He left his own servant behind and took a B.H.Q. servant to act as guide. I accompanied him as I wanted to visit my lot. Tatham smoked away at his pipe and at last, as we were plunging through mud and filth, he said 'This is what you might call the abomination of desolation, Padre.'

I saw Bartlett, the C.O., and McDougal in our B.H.Q., a dugout, and visited our men in their trenches. These were all newly dug but already very full of water. I went over to see Rose's (12th Sussex) men, also just dug in after a sort and still being consolidated. They were not very deep down. Some of the men were just standing with ground sheets over their shoulders and all the picture of misery, poor chaps. I gave them some cigarettes and told them to try and stick it. They had all had hard fighting and a rotten time. Rose was cheerful enough.

I found Thom (the Brigade's senior padre) and co. at the 14th Hants aid post and got back again somehow to Calf Support, having taken careful note of certain land-marks such as Kitchener's Wood [it *was* a wood, now just a few bare blasted stumps of trees], and now know my way if we go again.

1 August. Gatchell and five dressers and I moved on to Canopers Trench where Thom was yesterday. On the way—Gatchell went very fast—I spied a large circular hammered gong hanging outside a German dugout and collared it and hurried after the rest. I thought if I got through this stunt what an awfully nice thing it would be to take back to Madge [Murray's wife]. It kept hitting the mud as I carried it in my hand so I put the long cord it was hung by round my neck but it nearly strangled me.

We got to Canopers Trench at last over the most fearful country and through deep slime. It was a hottish journey in the way of fire but we were none of us hit. It was all out in the open in the sight of the Boche. Everybody went everywhere like that. I heard that this casual walking about by everybody—it was the only

thing to do, you could not follow the smashed trenches
—puzzled and flurried the Boche. There were people
everywhere and he did not know who to shoot at first. Of
course a lot did get hit.

At the Canopers Trench RAP we had not a very great
deal of work as we were no longer attacking but holding,
under appalling conditions, what we had taken—a 2 mile
advance at least, I believe, on a very long front. During
the day I visited the trench, or remains of it, in which we
all were and the men's rifles were all bunged up with mud
and everything was in a state of chaos. Still, there they
had got, and there they were. Several times we were told
that the Boche was coming in to a counter attack but he
could not get through the mud. Our machine gun fire
stopped him before he had got far.

That night five men, part of the crew of a big disabled
tank behind us, came in to the RAP as their captain had
told them they could clear out if they could reach the
trench. The tank was some shelter but was being shelled.
They had no food. Nor had we. I think they really came
because they were hungry and thirsty, though one was
wounded in the arm and we dressed him.

The night was wet (it was the rain that ruined the
complete success of the whole show) and we had a cold
wet hungry and generally rotten time. I thought we were
done for once or twice as the shelling was pitiless and
HOME seemed to recede into an impossibility. We had
none of us shaved since Sunday and looked awful sweeps.
A few wounded crawled in from time to time. No
stretcher could be carried in as the entrance was far too
narrow. We dressed broken legs etc. and put the men on
stretchers ready to be evacuated in a lean-to outside.
Then the lean-to was blown away and we had not even
got that.

One man groaned terribly but we got him evacuated at

last and I put my trench coat over him as it was raining very hard. I wonder if he got down safely across that hell behind us? I was almost as sorry for the stretcher bearers on a long night journey like that.

2 August. Our pioneers got ready two men for burial and I buried them just over the parapet. We had a fair amount of work to do but no water or food and there was now a foot of water in the pillbox. Sometime in the afternoon I was with the five dressers sitting in the pillbox on petrol tins with my haversack and gong near me, the latter being half under water against the concrete wall. We were trying to get a little rest and I was half asleep. Suddenly a most terrific noise and explosion took place and we were all knocked over and I felt a violent singing on a very high note in each ear, especially the left, all other sounds being very far away.

We got out or were got out somehow but I collapsed as soon as I stood up. I remember that I saw the faces of all the dressers who were alive. One had a cut on his forehead and another on his face. I noticed that my left legging had been ripped off by a piece of shell, as clean as if it had been done by a razor, from top to bottom. It fell off my leg when I attempted to walk. Two of the dressers took me along to B.H.Q. where Gatchell was and he ticketed me 'Wounded. Concussion.'

I remember resisting and being silly about wanting to stay on. Eventually the Adjutant sent me down with his own servant. I tore my ticket off my shoulder strap and told the Adjutant's servant that I must go back to the line and generally behaved like a baby. I expect it was the lack of food as well as the shell shock.

How we got down I do not know but that man was awfully good and gentle as well as strong. It was a nightmare walk. I remember the awful mud more than anything. The duckboards disappeared altogether in it.

There was a mule sinking fast in a shell hole full of mud. Only his head was out and two men were pulling at him. He kept throwing up his head to keep it out of the mud.

I remember also, near an approach to the Canal Bank, a sort of walking wounded halt where we were given hot Oxo and bully beef sandwiches. My goodness, how we did fall on that food, and didn't it taste good. Across the Canal Bank was a Field Ambulance where were three padres of our Division I knew, Scanlon, Nonconformist, Ross the R.C. and Topham, who were posted here and were all very kind to me.

I got into a horse ambulance with a lot of men and went to the Corps dressing station where Crawley and other padres were and there was a gramophone and hot tea and food. Here I was washed and put into some pyjamas (the Red Cross supply all these things), retaining my tunic, boots and breeches only, my tin hat, respirator etc. all being scrapped and taken away from me. I don't know what became of my haversack with all my belongings. It was a very good one. Also that gong must be in the wrecked pillbox still.

Murray spent a week at a Casualty Clearing Station (where, at his own request, he received Holy Communion on a Saturday morning, 'thinking by mistake that it was Sunday morning') before being put aboard an ambulance train for Boulogne as a stretcher case. Though his left ear was painful and discharging all the time, he evidently still felt guilty at being returned to Blighty:

Chaise, one of our 13th Sussex officers, was in a lower bunk near me. He had 10 wounds and was very bad. I could not help feeling what a lot of trouble I had given, and was giving, to my country over a burst eardrum compared with his injuries.

Even in his diary entry for the day he arrived back at Leybourne Rectory in the peace of the Kentish countryside, Murray is preoccupied with his experiences at the front. His expressions of respect, even sympathy, for the enemy echo those of numerous combatants who have written about the emotional gulf that existed between them and the Hun-hating civilian population.

22 August. Oh, it was nice to see Madge again. She looked very well, but thin. Joan and Betty, I learned, are at Wicken. We had a long talk about everything and she told me all about home things and showed me the garden. It looked perfect, the apple and plum crop was marvellous. Hayes, the new gardener, seems very good. He was interested to hear about the front and seemed almost horrified to hear that we had tended almost as many Boche as our own men in the aid posts.

There is far less hatred of Germany in the front line than at home I think. Here I suppose he is a sort of bogey such as 'Boney' was in the Napoleonic wars—hated because unseen. He is really not too bad and a great fighter and Methodist. We were always struck by the extreme pallor of German prisoners and their expressionless faces. Our men looked redder and spryer altogether and less heavy. It was a kind of 'student' look that many Germans had. I could not wish to meet more diligent men than those Prussians who carried for us at the beginning of the advance. Their unquestioning and doglike obedience was also remarkable and told a tale of very good discipline.

While I remember it all it is worth perhaps recording also, for Joan and Betty to read someday, that the patience and sort of self-effacement and almost apologetic attitude of the prisoners struck me very much and awoke pity. Their attitude was almost as if they would say 'It *is* rather surprising that we have been taken and a nuisance to us and to you. We are sorry to trouble you. Don't mind us, we will help all we can.' Their gratitude for food and cigarettes was very deep.

After three weeks Murray's ear had almost healed and he was pronounced fit to return to the front. He got back to Brigade headquarters on 13 September:

Very nice to be back. They all chaffed me about my wound stripe which they called 'the padre's stair rod'. Thom was wearing a bar to his M.C. and I congratulated him. He appears to get some decoration after every fight and I know enough of him to be sure he deserves it, and *the men say so* which is the best guide of all. He said, which was surprising news to me, that I was recommended for the M.C. after the last advance but that 'no one gets it first time' . . .

There was a lull in the battle, though the guns still blazed on both sides. On a visit with Thom to the front, on 17 September, Murray was given a lesson on misplaced courage by his admired superior:

. . . Just where a narrow gauge line, used for stores, wounded, shells etc., branches to the right near the Brick Stack Thom and I found five Gloucesters all dead on the tramway, still warm and bleeding from a shell which had just burst before we came round the corner. I couldn't leave them all there, blown to bits, and began to get them onto the truck which they had been wheeling when they were killed. I think I meant to wheel them away and bury them but Thom stopped me when I had got three onto the truck and he forced me to hurry on saying 'It is no use. This is out of our area and not our job and where one shell fell another will come. What's the good of a dead padre to anyone?'

I thought it was our job, as the Gloucesters are our divisional pioneers, but Thom knows best and *never risks his own or others' lives for dead men but as much as you like for living ones.* This is sound, and Thom is a very great man over appreciating values and acting promptly on all occasions. One trusts him absolutely. So I left them as he advised. There were men all round us and it would all be attended to by the proper people in time . . .

Ironically it was the burying of the dead that occupied much of Murray's time, and put him at greatest risk, during his next spell in the front line. This was during a comparative lull between what became known as the First and Second Battles of Passchendaele.

16 October to 19 October: I lived in the R.A.P. burying dead by day when possible and visiting trenches and Battalion H.Q. Our unit buried about 100. I was in charge of a burying party of 8. I was told to bury for choice between 7 and 9 a.m. 'in the mist', and if shelling took place to take the men in, and not to look like a 'working party' if avoidable, and other good advice.

I may as well state how I organised my little party in this sad but necessary work. We all had spades. The corporal and I went first, looking for dead. They were not difficult to find as a rule and special groups of dead had been reported to me, also just where they lay, and with special instructions to bury those recently killed on or near the duck board track to the front line. These men had been killed during the night or perhaps several nights before, going into or coming out of the line, ration carrying etc. etc. It must be understood that the whole of this country is pitted with shell holes of from 3 ft. to 20 ft. in diameter, the older ones being full of water.

I kept the 6 other men back with instructions to keep us in sight and to advance after us 2 by 2 and each file to be

25 yds. from the next. As soon as I found a body (some in the older disused trenches were terribly decomposed and had been out for months by all appearances) I dragged it, with the corporal, into the nearest new, or recent, shell hole, after searching the body and putting all belongings into a small ration of canvas bag and writing name, unit number etc. in indelible ink on the outside of the bags (I stuffed my tunic pockets with these canvas bags before sallying out) and then said the Committal words of the Prayer Book Burial Service and these additional words for the benefit of the corporal and for my own or anyone who might be present—'Lord, we thank Thee for the example of this brave man who gave his life for his country. Grant him eternal rest and so teach us to number *our* days that we may apply our hearts unto wisdom. Amen.'

Then I and the corporal each placed 12 spades full of earth (only it was always mud up there) on the body, and beckoning to the next 2 men who would be hidden in a shell hole 25 yards away, went on to the next body. The 2 men behind shovelled 24 spadesful between them and so we went on. The place was marked on the map and correct map references made afterwards in reserve. The manner of marking such graves is either to place the man's tin hat on a reversed rifle or to put a rifle alone in the ground—there are always heaps of rifles about—or to put his name on a piece of paper in an empty bottle, neck down and corked with something. Sometimes a rough cross can be made if there is time and opportunity, either from the various pieces of rivetting timber or of iron tied together with telegraph wire. It is surprising what a lot of odd pieces of iron and telegraph wire there are about on a battlefield.

Later, when the area becomes 'quiet', the G.R.U. will come and put up their little official crosses with the man's

name, number, unit and date of death, or date of burial if
the latter was not ascertainable, on a strip of zinc stamped
with capital letters just as you stamp your name in the
penny-in-the-slot machines at home.

At 9 on Friday night, October 19th, we were relieved.
We all got down safely, I to Beggar's Rest. Our losses
were heavy though we only held the line for five days.

Between then and 30 November, the 'official' conclusion
to the Third Battle of Ypres, Murray was in and out of the
line. He makes no mention of the progress of the battle,
wholly concerned with the welfare of his 'parish'. These are
typical excerpts:

. . . Went overland to the Menin Road. This road was
fearfully knocked about and there were a good many not
very recent dead along it. I had taken 500 Woodbines and
Gold Flake with me and gave them to any men I saw in
the trenches. In one deep sandy trench I saw a man who
had been buried and could not be got out. Also the black
head of another man sticking out of the side of the trench
quite low down at the bottom. I was told nearly everybody stumbles and trips over it at night. They found him
when digging the trench and did not like to interfere with
the head . . .

. . . Parade service in two sets for 13th Sussex near
some fallen logs at Beggar's Rest. Two Lewis guns
mounted at each service and only 50 men allowed to
collect at a time according to order. The men sat on the
fallen logs during the sermon. I preached on 'Thankfulness' . . .

. . . I could not sleep much. At 6 a.m. a most terrific
drum fire was set up by us. I do not know why or what it
all meant though mention was made of a big advance,
probably on our left. It began to rain and continued all
morning. The others, the doctor, dressers and wounded,

all slept on. I read a boys' story called 'The Taming of the Third' . . .

. . . In the evening I drew my 'lightning sketches' at a Brigade concert at the YMCA. A poor show but Bothal-my, I thought, sang very well. He was at Magdalen, Oxford, when he joined up. They seemed to like my poor efforts—a new one was 'The Pill Box'. I thought Chester of the 11th was rather an ass to dress up a private as a girl and pretend to kiss him (or her) in 'If you were the only girl in the world' . . .

. . . Coming back by lorry we were held up by a New Zealand Division moving up to the line for the first time. A very fine lot of men indeed. I found myself reflecting upon the steady, stately advance of that Division into the great danger zone and of their service to be done there for the old Empire, of money, brains, trouble, attention to detail, training etc., and then the advance at last into the real thing. One thought of the homes and people of those men so far away, also of the utter pity of it all—but finally of the glory of it that men were still men and willing to do men's great work . . .

. . . Slept well after asking God to show His power in some way in this war 1) for His Honour and Glory 2) to convince and convert unbelieving people and 3) to confirm the faithful. Prayed this very long and earn-estly . . .

. . . I am reading 'A Garland of Thoughts', being extracts from good poetry and prose. One needs some-thing of that out here very much. One gets fed up with things like La Vie Parisienne, the London Magazine and the flood of pictures of half naked women pinned up in the messes . . .

. . . Had cocoa and biscuits at a YMCA hut and talked to the elderly 'conductor'. He confessed, in answer to a question of mine, that as far as his experience went, the spiritual life of the YMCA out here was practically nil. I reassured him by saying that the 'cup of cold water' (to say nothing of hot cocoa) would not be forgotten on earth and might be remembered in Heaven . . .

There is no indication in Murray's diary that he was aware when a halt was called to the battle. But eight days later, on 28 November, he found himself for the first time amid the ruins of the medieval city in and around which there had been such carnage ever since British and French troops had entered and occupied it in October 1914.

. . . Ypres is an astounding sight, hopelessly battered, soldiers everywhere and all ruins tenanted. The doctor and I are in a dugout in the corridor of the Convent, near to Brigade H.Q. I wonder whether the people who knew Ypres in 1914, '15, '16 or even during this summer when we were on the Canal Bank and shells were raining on the town in thousands, would ever have believed that a time would come when an average of only 12 shells a day would fall on the town (for such is the average). Ypres at present has become as bon a spot as one could find in the Salient . . .

All was now relatively quiet on the Ypres front as a freezing winter set in. The aftermath of battle is evoked by Murray in a paragraph tucked away at the end of a typically lengthy and matter-of-fact entry, on 3 December. A haunting little cameo, reminiscent of his descriptions of the train journey to the front, it hints at another side to his nature than that of extrovert padre.

. . . I noticed how beautiful the winter afterglow was viewed from inside the lorry I rode in this evening, I being up at the driver's end and looking back to Poperinghe. The horizon was misty grey, there up higher dull red, then orange, then primrose and finally a cold azure blue. There was one aeroplane only, going 'home' to Proven. Camp fires gleamed out of the gloom. Endless streams of six-horse limbers and lorries. The trees stalked onto my little stage, meeting in a brown-grey haze with ultramarine distance. One of the two gunners who were sitting at the end of the lorry had a fine profile. I wish I could have drawn and painted the little movie show in its semicircular setting from under the hood of the lorry . . .

Christmas Day found Murray far from the front line in the village of Coulomby, where the Brigade was billeted for a rest period. It was snowing. He had received a letter from Madge—'She wished I could help to hang up the children's stockings and said that Joan and Betty had been very busy shouting to Father Christmas up the chimney, also writing notes to him.'
There was a lively dinner at the mess that night.

The C.O. sang 'Old King Cole'. The King and the C.O. were the only toasts but the C.O. added me very kindly and called me a 'pukka padre'. I thanked them and was asked to propose 'absent friends', of course this meant all who had been killed as well as those at home, so there was a special reason for drinking it standing up and in silence.

Earlier, after conducting a church parade service, Murray had paid a visit to the Band.

I lent them my 'Camp Songs'. Later on I heard them playing 'Oh who will o'er the downs with me'—a tune which lays hold of me for some reason. It always to me suggests mystery and passionate longing and adventure . . .

Adventure, mystery, longing—were such feelings, as much as a Christian's desire to serve others, at the back of Murray's mind when he badgered his bishop to be sent to the front? Certainly there is a note of nostalgia in his brief description of his farewell visit to the Ypres Salient five days before the completion of his contract and his return to the uneventful life of a country parson.

8 January 1918. Heavy snow in night. I had a snow bath in the morning. Tramped and lorried with Collinson to Hill Top. Camps now all over what used to be No Man's Land last June. It seems so funny to be able to walk about openly in places where there was nothing but wire and thistles and you had to dodge about like a rabbit with a weasel after it. It was somewhere up here that Piper and I used to go up the line together, keeping low in the bad places . . .

It was as a country parson (with a special interest in the British Legion and village sporting activities) that Murray spent the rest of his working life, most of it as Rector of Chulmleigh in North Devon. He died in 1943 at the age of 73.

'My father had a very active happy life, absorbed in everything he did,' says Mrs Joan Roberts, eldest of three daughters (the youngest was born in 1919). 'He loved people and got on with anyone, regardless of class or religion. As a parson he saw his main work as visiting villagers in their homes, whether churchgoers or not. He was a most generous man, though never well off—I remember my mother being a little annoyed on one occasion when he gave a brand new suit to someone in need.'

Mrs Roberts was talking at her home near Pulborough, Sussex. In a place of honour in the oak-beamed, open-hearthed sitting room rested the silver cigarette box, engraved with the Sussex Regimental crest, presented to her father at a farewell concert on the eve of his departure from France. She was only six at the time and has only a vague recollection of his homecoming. What surprises her now is that she cannot recall her father ever talking about his experiences at the front. Though she knew that a diary existed, it was only recently that it came to light and she read it for the first time, discovering that she and her sister Betty were very much in her father's mind when he wrote it.

When I was typing it out in 1977 to send to the Imperial War Museum, it was like hearing him talk again. I was moved by little things, like his references to giving his 'lightning sketch' act at camp concerts. This was the act he used to do at village concerts—drawings on large sheets of paper that depicted something else when turned upside down. His reference to trying out a soldier's rifle and pack on a route march reminded me of an occasion when he walked 22 miles from Chulmleigh to Exeter because he wanted to know what tramps felt like on the road—there was a constant stream of vagrants in those days and they could always rely on his generosity.

Mrs Roberts feels, nonetheless, that the diary does less than justice to her father's personality.

You would not gather from it that he had a marvellous sense of humour—I remember him as being so funny, doing crazy things. And his love of people does not really come across. I am sure he got closer to the Tommies than the diary suggests. His reticence on the religious side does not surprise me—he never tried to pump religion into anyone.

It was as a veteran of the First World War that her late husband Robbie viewed the diary (he married Joan in 1958 and never knew his father-in-law). Roberts volunteered in 1916 at the age of 15 (giving a false age) and served throughout the Battle of the Somme with a machine gun company. After being wounded in January 1917 he was at a general hospital in

Rouen just about the time Padre Murray was settling in. Said Roberts:

> There is no doubt that my father-in-law must have gone through some very harrowing times on the Ypres front and I am not at all surprised that he never talked about them. My own experiences were so awful that I tried to block them from my mind. It was not until the 1950s that I started to get interested in what had happened and to read up about the war.

Though himself brought up in a God-fearing family ('four services on Sundays, family prayers and grace at every meal'), Roberts recalled that he was like most Tommies at the front in having little time for organised religion.

> During training I could not quite connect what the padre was lecturing us about with being taught the best way of getting a bayonet in and out. When I got to France I told myself 'I'm out here to do a job, and a bloody awful job, and I want nothing to do with church—I'll live by my own religion'. Though I never personally met a padre at the front, they were generally regarded as a bit of a joke—'Here's the old Sky Pilot'.

For his father-in-law, both from what he had read in the diary and from what he had learned about him from family and friends, Roberts had formed the greatest respect and admiration. But, though agreeing with his wife that his compassion for others and his generous spirit must have had full play on the battlefield, he had his own interpretation of the diary. 'He was a man of action, energetic, very fit, interested in all that was going on,' he said. 'I think he would have liked to have been a fighting man.'

CHAPTER FIVE

THE OLD SCHOOL DOG-COLLAR

As a public school chaplain, the Rev Victor Tanner took like a duck to water to an officers' mess on the Western Front in the spring of 1916. The Battle of the Somme, which was to decimate the 'flower of England', lay ahead. It was still taken for granted that an officer was a product of the public schools. The youngest of the subalterns Tanner now encountered were only one remove from the schoolboy cadets to whom he had until recently been directing his patriotic homilies in the chapel of Weymouth College. He felt at home with them.

'The officers just regard the Padre as one of themselves,' Tanner wrote in his diary at the Machine Gun Corps base depot at Camiers (where he was to spend the first nine months of his 3½ years as a padre). 'I have not heard a single taunt levelled against religion since I came here, and, more interesting still, one scarcely ever hears bad language or risqué stories. If it should happen at any time it is usually accompanied with an "Excuse me, Padre" . . .'

But with the Battle of the Somme, this cosy, elitist atmosphere, in which an Anglican padre's dog-collar could almost be equated with the old school tie, began to dissipate. Some time after the offensive had been launched, Tanner wrote:

The 'Push' is certainly having its effect down here for draft after draft is coming from England. One thing that depresses me more than any other is the change in the character and attitude of the new officers. When I first came we had a wonderful lot, very friendly and helpful in every way. These new chaps are quite different. Many of them are not merely indifferent to religion but openly anti-religious. One, whom I heard using the most disgraceful language the other day, went up the Line a day or two later and was killed soon after he had got into the trenches . . .

Though Tanner does not mention it, it was class as much as attitudes to religion that made the difference. The 'new chaps' coming out as replacements were among the first to have been commissioned from the ranks, without benefit of public school, university or Sandhurst. They came from the lower middle class or working class, and for them the public school ethos, so closely linked with the Church of England, went for little. The days when a mess could be relied on to provide the exclusive company of 'officers and gentlemen' were numbered. By the end of the war only a third of officers were public school men: the rest had been promoted from the ranks.

There are no further disparaging references in Tanner's diary to this new breed of officer, though in the summer of 1917 he does describe a week spent at a Chaplains' School at St Omer as 'such a delightful change from the atmosphere and conversation of the Mess'. Most of the diary is concerned with his duties among the Tommies and the dangers he shared with them. His avowed aim had been 'to be with the men at this their time of deepest need', and 'to build up what I hope will be a new conception of the parson after the war'. His dedication to the former aim is testified to by the fact that he was awarded the M.C. for his part in the Battle of

Passchendaele in 1917 and a bar to the M.C. during the German offensive in the spring of 1918. About general attitudes to the parson after the war he was scarcely in a position to judge. Up to his retirement as a public school chaplain and housemaster in 1951, and even beyond that to his death in 1977 at the age of 91, Tanner, a bachelor, cosily confined himself to school, village and countryside pursuits.

For the purposes of this book Tanner's diary is of particular interest in being so directly rooted in that ethos from which stemmed so much of the 'God on our side' propaganda of the time. It was in the school chapel that most of those now in positions of authority, whether in politics, the services or the church, had been indoctrinated with the ideals of patriotism and Christianly behaviour—loyalty, devotion to duty, self-sacrifice, self-discipline—and equipped with the flowery language in which to project them.

As much as anything it was the high-flown language of the Anglican padre, so divorced from the stark realities of the trenches, that set him apart from the Tommy. The few examples of Tanner's sermons that have been preserved are typical. The didactic tone remains the same whether he is urging the boys of Weymouth College to give God their 'fullest cooperation' in defence of the right, or, as a padre, likening a compulsory church parade to 'a weekly Spiritual kit inspection, when the Divine Quartermaster comes to see if we have the spiritual equipment that we need, to enquire whether we have been drawing our daily ration of strength, to show us anything in our "kit" which we would be better without.' It is even there in the morass of the Ypres Salient when he is addressing the survivors of his regiment shortly after the Battle of Passchendaele, on the unlikely text 'Bless the Lord, O my soul, and forget not all His benefits':

. . . Many have passed through the veil which hides us from the great spiritual world. Bravely they fought and nobly they died in the greatest and most sacred cause in which men have ever taken up arms, and humanity will for ever bless their memory. For them we need not mourn. Death is like the drawing aside of a veil and passing from one room to another. A nobler activity is theirs today, greater opportunities for the development of character and a sphere of wider usefulness, as we Christians firmly believe . . .

The concept of heaven as a kind of celestial college of further education is in keeping with Tanner's character as well as calling. He was imbued all his life with a sense of duty and service, and never more so than in the years as a padre he documented at such length. How seriously he took his role is clear from a letter he wrote to his widowed mother before the Battle of Passchendaele, to be posted only in the event of his death. In it he gives as his reasons for 'going up into this fight voluntarily and of my own free will' not only that he feels his presence may be of help to 'these brave Worcestershire lads', but 'because the honour of Christ's church is entrusted to us Chaplains and we must not be wanting of so great a privilege.'

Two matching pairs of snapshots of Tanner in uniform underline this sense of high resolve. Marked 'Summer' and 'Winter', two were taken on leaves from the front in the garden of his mother's home near Winchester, two 'in the line'. The pose is almost identical, left hand on hip, right hand clutching his cane. One can picture him in just such a stance in the uniform of Scoutmaster, a role he had played with equal dedication at Weymouth College.

One might get the impression from such photographs, as from some of the diary entries, that Tanner was a bit of a prig. In fact he had been one of the most popular members of the staff at Weymouth College, and after the war came to be loved as well as respected at the two public schools he served over a span of 36 years. From the tributes paid to him, by old boys and staff alike, he emerges as a real life 'Mr Chips', nurturing and cherishing through generations of boys the same traditions and ideals, a scholastic father figure. In reading the diary, a mostly factual account of his day-to-day experiences as a padre, one must take on trust the endearing qualities of warmth and humour he was to be remembered by.

Born in 1886, educated at Dean Close School, Cheltenham, and Cambridge, Tanner was ordained in 1909 and appointed chaplain to Weymouth College in 1912, where he also taught history and divinity in the Junior School and ran the Scout pack and College Field Club. Although he offered his services as a padre as soon as war was declared, he had to wait until a replacement could be found for him as school chaplain. He relates how the war first made a direct impact on the school:

> In June 1915 the news came through that one of the most popular boys, Louis Broome (Chummy), who only left the school for Sandhurst 4 months before the outbreak of the war, had been killed by a sniper in France. Broome and Palmer had been bosom friends at school, had shared the captaincy and vice-captaincy of most games and were invariably spoken of together. Palmer, after one leave during which he visited the school, was himself killed in the following year. By the time the war ended the school's Roll of Honour contained no less than 94 names —92 boys, 2 masters.

It was on 2 April 1916 that Tanner preached his farewell sermon in the school chapel, embarking for France two weeks later. Two letters written to him by a master in charge of the school's O.T.C. are revealing, not only in establishing the high regard in which he was held, but in hinting at the darker side of public school life.

. . . Needless to say you are jolly well missed here. One never hears a single nasty thing about you, which is 'some' testimony at a place like a school where scandal is rife. I think you did a jolly sporting game in leaving, since there was plenty of excuse for your staying on and having the comfortable life here . . . I am getting on fairly well with the boys at present but am always liable to drop bricks through a lack of thought. The ordinary boys I have no trouble with, but the prefects at times forget themselves and have to be let into . . .

. . . I can tell you that we miss you here, directly as well as indirectly from what we hear from the Junior School. The Scouts do not get on as well as under your control by a long chalk . . . Ritson gave us a capital bombing display yesterday—sort of things that kill at 200 yards so we had to be jolly careful. I have 60 in the Corps at present. A great idea at the end of this term is a camp in the school grounds for a few days—hope it will go off alright—the Head rather afraid of various things but I am being careful to arrange the tents so as to avoid risk as far as possible. There are not many inclined that way fortunately. I wish I had you here to help as I am sure you would . . .

In 1917 a sensation was caused by the publication of Alec Waugh's *Loom of Youth*, based on his recent schooldays at Sherborne. 'Half the housemasters in the country found their desks littered with letters from anxious parents demanding an assurance that their Bobbie was not subject to the temptations described in this alarming book,' Waugh wrote in a later introduction. 'No book before had accepted as part of the fabric of school life the inevitable emotional consequences of monastic herding together for 8 months of the year of 13-year old children and 18-year old adolescents.'

For Tanner, immersed in his padre's duties, such problems

had paled into insignificance. Though he spent part of every leave at Weymouth College, there are few other references to the school in his diary. Among the earlier ones he records having located the grave of Louis Broome (for whom he had conducted a memorial service in the school chapel) and laid on it a wreath of geraniums in the form of a cross, and of being about to go to the moral aid of another old boy of much less exemplary character:

> I had a phone message last night saying that an old Weymouth College boy had turned up at the Machine Gun School for the course. It so happens that I had a long letter from the Headmaster's wife about that very boy only a month ago, saying that he had gone badly off the rails and was about to go over to France. She hoped I would be able to contact him. How wonderfully God works . . .

But it was the Tommy who now absorbed much of his endeavours. As first chaplain of the newly-formed Machine Gun Corps at Camiers, he instituted regular church parades, services and Bible talks, equipping a church tent with chairs, portable organ, red-white-and-blue carpet in front of the altar and Union Jack above the Communion table. His anxiety to become accepted as a good sport, as well as a spiritual adviser, is indicated in some of the following representative extracts:

> What a privilege it is to be here amongst these men at this their time of deepest need. I was asked especially to go to see a man in No. 4 Hospital. He turned out to be quite a young chap. The lad greeted me with a beaming smile, despite the fact that his right arm had just been taken off. His right leg was also broken above the knee and his shoulder blade broken. Poor chap, he had had his share and a great deal more but his cheerfulness was marvel-

lous. His chief concern was for his mother. He is dreading going home for her sake . . .

I am getting to know the men by degrees. One young chap came up to me in the YMCA Hut and said 'I've been thinking lately, Sir, that I ought to turn over a new leaf. Something that you said on Easter Sunday has set me thinking.' We had a long talk and then went into the Church Tent and, as we knelt together at the Communion Rails, he dedicated himself to Christ . . .

. . . I give a couple of hours each day to the censoring of the men's letters and could not help noticing a remark which one man made in his letter to his wife, who had evidently asked the name of the Chaplain. 'No' he wrote 'I don't know his name but he's a nice chap and gets about amongst the men as much as possible. Sometimes he comes on a route march with us. I think we all like him' . . .

. . . One young chap came up to me the other day and said that he was worried at finding himself getting into the drinking and gambling habit. I had a talk with him which he seemed to appreciate. He promised to come along to the Sunday Bible talk . . .

. . . Went up to the Range today with several of the officers and at their invitation had an hour's revolver and rifle shooting! I did better than I expected and shall certainly go again . . .

The tennis court is now nearly ready for use. It is going to be a great boon to young officers coming down the Line for a rest. I feel that it is a good thing to take part in these and similar activities, as it may build up what I hope will be a new conception of the parson after the war, namely that he is as human as anyone else and that he takes just as much interest in the ordinary things of life, but, with it, he tries, albeit very imperfectly, to put spiritual things first . . .

. . . The towns and villages swarm with children, friendly little things who come up to one, stand at attention and salute as they have seen the British Tommies do. Some go further and take one's hand or run alongside saying 'Pen-ny, pen-ny'. Nearly all French boys of 7 or 8 years smoke and frequently use swear words learnt from our men . . .

. . . I spend a good deal of time going round the men's tents in the evening and, as a rule, I find them very friendly and ready for a chat . . .

In January 1917 Tanner was transferred to the 100th Brigade and attached to the 2nd Worcester Regiment (with whom he was to serve until his demobilisation in 1919). The long-awaited chance to 'be where the lads are and to share their experiences—and their dangers' had come. And for him, as his diary entry at the time reveals, there was nothing over-inflated in the conviction that the challenge was of God's making and that, in sharing those dangers, he would be following directly in the steps of Jesus Christ:

I shall be awfully sorry in many ways to leave Machine Guns, where I have been so happy, but I am sure that I am in the line of God's will. My Mother will, I am afraid, be very anxious and worried but I have written to try and cheer her up. As I tell her, my work in life has been planned out by God and therefore my times are in His hands.

I have often thought lately of the Gospel incident recorded by St John, when Jesus announced His intention of going into a district where His life had previously been threatened. His disciples did their utmost to dissuade Him from going because of the danger involved, but to no purpose. 'Are there not twelve hours in the day?' He said. 'As long as a man walketh in the day he stumbleth not.' A set time in which to do it. Nothing can happen to him until the 'twelve hours' is completed.

That this reliance on a divine dispensation was at the root of Tanner's faith is clear from a footnote Tanner wrote to this entry in the typescript copy of the diary he prepared during his retirement. 'The constant recollection of this saying of Jesus acted as an inspiration to me all through my overseas service' he wrote. 'Each man has his divinely appointed "Day"—his "Twelve hours"—in which to perform the life task which God has given him. As long as that task remains unfinished nothing untoward can happen to him. This thought relieved me of all sense of anxiety and fear.'

During the next eight months, when he saw action on the Somme and Arras fronts, Tanner's 'task' was the routine task of padres at the front—visiting men in their dugouts, burying the dead and writing to their relatives, assisting with the wounded, conducting services, organising facilities at rest camps. Two entries stand out as touchingly revealing the man behind the padre's uniform, a bachelor of 31, separated by the fortunes of war from those dearest to him, his recently widowed mother and only sister, on a day that should have been a family festivity:

9 April. The problem of getting home for my sister Dorothy's Wedding is exercising my mind considerably. I think the chances are small as the 'Push' has already begun and we may expect to be in the midst of it by the end of the week. I have written a long letter of congratulations and have sent her a cheque for £60 with which to buy a Piano when she is able to settle down in a home of her own. I told her she must not expect to see me on the day. It will be a bitter disappointment to her as well as to my Mother and it is a great trial to me.

14 April. Wedding Day. Whoever thought that the wedding would take place under such circumstances as

these. It looks as if we shall be in action very soon. By midday we had packed up and were awaiting the actual order to move. As the hour fixed for the Wedding drew near (2 p.m.) I strolled away from the Camp, found shelter from the wind in a shell-hole and read the Service slowly through. It seemed to bring me very near to her and gave me the opportunity of making the two Benedictions a real prayer for her and Arthur.

An altogether lighter-hearted picture of Tanner emerges from his description of the twelve days he spent in early September billeted at a château in the village of Hellebroucq behind Ypres. His regiment, which had moved up towards the Salient, where the Third Battle of Ypres had been launched a month before, had commandeered half the château as Headquarters Mess. In the other half lived an Anglo-French family, with two pretty daughters and two sons, described by Tanner as 'just like English public-school boys—full of life and merriment, with charming personalities'.

Billeted with Tanner were the Colonel of the Regiment, the Battalion Major, the Adjutant and the Doctor. Among the attractions for visiting officers from the nearby village (the two pretty daughters apart) were a stream with a punt, a tennis court, a billiards room and stables. Tanner himself had no need of the latter, having recently acquired from the Colonel a black mare called 'Satan', about which he comments 'The great problem seems to be to find out whether the Church will succeed in establishing itself on Satan or whether Satan will disestablish the Church!'

Like that 'sound of revelry by night' on the eve of Waterloo, the festivities and flirtations of this château interlude were apparently unclouded by the menace of the distant gunfire from one of history's bloodiest battlefields. A sunlit snapshot of a four-in-hand, packed with officers and ladies sporting floppy hats and sunshades, driving off from the château for a day out at a Divisional Horse Show, could be in a peacetime setting. And rarely has the bachelor padre, though more observer than participant, appeared in higher spirits.

6 September. We are getting to know the family at the Chateau quite well now. We had a dance this evening. As very few of us menfolk could dance at all we got a good deal of fun out of it. Adjutant Fox, however, is a really good dancer. The Colonel amused everyone by arranging a little sitting-out corner for two, carefully screened from view by a palm! . . .

12 September. Barker and Ward's visits to our Chateau are of very frequent occurrence just now and the reason is not far to seek. Barker seems certainly very enamoured of Betty. Ward tries hard to amuse and please all and succeeds in pleasing none! The most humorous attachment of all is that which has sprung up between Green (our youngest officer) and a young girl who is staying with the family. The punt proves of great attraction for all these couples. We all had tea on the lawn today with the family . . .

13 September. Celebrated our last day in these delightful surroundings by having a big dinner party and inviting the family. As there were not enough ladies to go round the youngest boy, Jean, was dressed up as Miss Celia Smith! The table was prettily decorated and we had a good menu: Hors d'oeuvres, Tomato Soup, Plaice, Chicken, Fruit Salad, Custard, Dessert, Coffee. Major Pardoe's game of guessing the identity of various objects which were passed round under the table provoked a great deal of amusement. When the chicken's foot and the suede glove soaked in water and stuffed with hay was passed round the ladies uttered wild shrieks! The rest of

the evening was spent in listening to music in the drawing-room or dancing in the billiard room.

15 September. The Battalion marched off, most of the
inhabitants coming out to see us off. The whole family
came from the Chateau and Omer, the eldest boy, took
several snapshots as we marched past. Major Pardoe, the
Battalion C.O., the Doc and I were mounted and rode
behind the Companies. We were led by the Battalion
band. It has done much to help the morale of the men at
critical times, and this was certainly one of them, as we all
had the instinctive feeling that we are in for a difficult and
dangerous job . . .

It was back to the serious business of war. A week later
Tanner was conducting a 'Pre-Battle Service' in a Church
Army chapel. The crowded congregation sang 'Jesu, lover of
my soul', 'Through the night of doubt and sorry', 'Through
all the changing scenes of life' and 'Soldiers of Christ arise'.
Tanner took as the theme of his sermon the Lord God's
exhortation to Joshua before the crossing of the river Jordan
('Be strong and of a good courage; be not afraid, neither be
thou dismayed . . .'). After the service numbers stayed for
Holy Communion. 'It was a wonderful time,' Tanner comments, 'and if ever I have been conscious of the "Real Presence" it was at the "Service before Action" this night.'

For Tanner the forthcoming battle was undoubtedly the
most momentous occasion of his life. Some 50 years later,
after rereading the letter he had written to his mother, to be
posted only in the event of his death, he added a note:

This letter must be typical of hundreds and indeed
thousands left behind at 'B' Echelon to be distributed
when necessary after the action. To me this is the most
sacred relic that I have of those war-time days. Anyone
reading it is (to me) treading on holy ground.

As earlier indicated, the letter is imbued with a spirit of dedication, and couched in the language familiar from his sermons:

. . . Death is no horror to me. As the entrance into a fuller and more useful life I look forward to it, though one would not be human if one did not shrink from the actual ordeal. Even the Master shrank for a moment in Gethsemane but He won the day . . . I have dedicated myself to my Master's work and nothing can happen to me unless my earthly task is done . . . In laying down my life I am offering *your* gift in the service of mankind . . .

More poignantly direct is the letter he wrote at the same time to his recently married sister:

Just a farewell word to you my darling. My letter to Mother will give you a general idea of what has been passing through my mind and therefore I will not trouble to repeat it here. What I do want to do is to thank you from my heart for all the happiness you have brought into my life. May the Master reward you by giving you a long married life of unalloyed happiness. That Arthur will be the best of husbands to you I cannot doubt. I know full well what you will be to him.

   Look after Mother for me won't you? This is the best tribute that you will be able to pay to my memory. In that wonderful life into which, if you receive this letter, I shall have entered, I shall be with Father and need you doubt that our thoughts and prayers will be with Mother, you and Arthur. So AU REVOIR, my darling, until that happy Easter morning of reunion.
   Ever your devoted brother, Victor.

The three-day battle (25–27 September) in which the 2nd Worcesters were engaged, and in which Tanner distinguished himself for his 'gallant and self-sacrificing conduct', was one of the many attempts to storm the Passchendaele Ridge that foundered in the mud before it was finally captured some six weeks later. The Worcesters, who succeeded in capturing the village of Gheluveld on the Menin Road, suffered 342 casualties before they were relieved.

Throughout the battle, a total of 72 hours, Tanner was posted in a German concrete pillbox, with an observation tower at the side, where he shared one of the ten small rooms with the Battalion M.O. and members of the Aid Post staff. It had been captured only three days before and was 'in a filthy and verminous condition—the whole place reeked'. The Germans, against whom a liquid flame-thrower had been used, had left behind a quantity of medical stores, which were put to ready use as the floor of the Aid Post became 'just one mass of mutilated, writhing humans'.

Tanner's most graphic account of his experiences is in the long letter he wrote to his mother two weeks after the engagement, based on notebook jottings at the time and the diary entries he expanded them into later. There is room here only for extracts, starting with a critical moment in the early stages when the Germans launched an attack.

. . . The Boche knew that we had planned our attack so thought he would strike first with the result that at dawn on the 26th he put over a terrific barrage. Our pillbox and observation tower were the main target.

The attack was so strong that the battalions on our right and left had been pressed back and from the Aid Post we could see the Boche steadily advancing. He captured two whole companies of the battalion on our right. The news was rather disquieting and the C.O. became a bit alarmed. He said, however, that if our battalion was forced back too, he would defend our pillbox to the last. So he got every available man out into the trenches in front of us—cooks, runners, signallers, servants and a machine gun.

The Doc and I gravely discussed what we should do if the Boche reached the pillbox. I said that we ought to fight until they actually entered it and then we should surrender. He had a revolver which, contrary to regulations, he always carried, and I had a rifle which one of the wounded men had left behind. However, we did not have to resort to such extremes, for the battalion on our left counter-attacked and regained their line, and the remaining companies of the battalion on our right did the same. My battalion had stood firm all the time. It really was rather exciting to be within such an ace of a trip to Berlin. A British padre would have been quite a surprise for them . . .

The courage and devotion to duty for which Tanner was later awarded the M.C. are indicated by the next two extracts. The first relates to an occasion when Tanner left the pillbox, during a heavy bombardment, to encourage a group of Tommies in a nearby trench:

About 20 men were huddled there, for protection, frightened to death, so I talked to them and tried to liven them up a bit. I asked them what their wives and mothers would think if they could see them under these circumstances, and one man said, 'It would kill mine right out, I know.' I also dished out cigarettes all round to try to take their minds off things a bit and it succeeded fairly well.

Every time a shell came we all ducked of course and as soon as the fountains of earth had settled down I said 'All serene, heads up' and they seemed to get much more confident. But the shells were close. One took a chunk off the concrete just over our heads and burst about 4 yards away. Three big splinters hit me on the arm and shoulders at different times but none of them broke the skin. One piece knocked off the tin hat of a man next to me and the hat fell into the lap of the third man from him.

After another fell close I said 'Now, lads, I am going to ask you to do something which perhaps you have not done yet. I am going to ask you to close your eyes and pray that God will protect and keep the boys in the front line, and that He will extend the protection to us', and every man closed his eyes. We could scarcely hear one another's voices amid the whistling and bursting of the shells. But God heard those prayers. That very trench was blown in during the afternoon and several men were killed and wounded . . .

On one occasion, when congestion of the wounded in the aid post was so acute that new stretcher-cases were being dumped outside, Tanner decided to have one badly wounded man carried to an intermediate aid post in the rear. Shouldering their burden, he and three stretcher-bearers set off on a 1½-mile trek under shellfire.

That journey I shall never forget. The stretcher seemed like lead. It was the continual going up and down into shell-holes that made it seem heavier than it really was, and then to make matters worse we lost our direction, there being no landmarks to guide us. Still we kept steadily on. Every time we stopped to change ends the poor chap on the stretcher would say 'Oh, don't bury me here. Do go on. We shall all be killed'—and so on.

I cannot describe the variety of feelings which I had during that journey, but somehow or other I did not feel a bit frightened. I suppose that I felt that it rested on me to keep up the spirits of the other three. I knew too that we were in the path of our duty, and therefore under God's immediate care.

Well at last we reached our destination and I shall never forget the gratitude which the poor chap showed us as we handed him over to the relay bearers. He wrung my hand

and burst into tears. 'I shall never forget you, Sir, you have saved my life' . . .

The closest Tanner gets to communicating the horrors of the battlefield is in a brief passage copied from notes he jotted down in the congested aid post during the afternoon of 26 September:

One young King's Royal Rifle Corps man had his face lacerated and caked with blood. All he could say was 'Shoot me, Doctor. Shoot me, please. Do shoot me.' He died soon after he left the Aid Post. Just inside the door was a man with a wrist broken and artery pierced by a splinter. Blood was pouring on the ground and a tourniquet had to be applied. Another young KRR man was lying on one side absolutely lacerated with splinter wounds. His tunic had been almost shot away. One man lay just inside the doorway unconscious. A bullet had pierced his brain. His papers showed that he was an R.C.

But the worst of all were the shell shock cases which came in. One big powerful Highlander was absolutely demented—shouting at the top of his voice the most utter nonsense and waving his arms and legs. One man, who was quite obviously too old to see active service, hung about all day in the doorway trembling from head to foot. We could not persuade him to go down the Line, try as hard as we could. Two others, quite young boys, were shaking from head to foot and cowering down every time a shell came over.

Of all of this there is never a hint in the 'bravely they fought and nobly they died' oration Tanner delivered to the survivors three days later. One can only speculate as to what their thoughts were as they listened to their padre, who had so recently been one of them, revert to that pontifical, pulpit voice:

. . . What effect should the death of our comrades have upon us? Surely it should strengthen our resolve to carry on without faltering till the object for which they died has been attained—England's honour vindicated, liberty established and a common brotherhood. When a feeling of war weariness comes over us, as it does from time to time, let us pray for the spirit of dogged perseverance and endurance. If God spares us to return home it must be our resolve to build a new England on the principles of righteousness, justice and brotherhood . . .

No pious platitudes accompanied another service Tanner conducted at this time. As 'representative of all those who had fallen in action', the body of the Battalion Adjutant had been chosen for ceremonial burial. This was that same Captain Fox whose prowess as a dancer Tanner had noted during that idyllic interlude in the château.

. . . The whole Battalion was formed up at 12.15 and the coffin, covered with the Union Jack, was carried slowly through the Camp between the men while the 'Drum' played a Funeral March. Six officers carried the body to the grave. We had no books but were able to sing 'Nunc Dimittis' and 'Jesus lover of my soul'. A brief pause after the Last Post had sounded brought to an end a most impressive Service—unique in my experience.

It was as something of a conquering hero that Tanner returned to Weymouth College to spend the last weekend of the winter term. He had recently received a letter from Elliot D. Forster, head boy of the Junior School: 'Just a line to congratulate you heartily on getting the M.C. It is ripping. I am a patrol-leader now, instead of a Wolf Cub. Quite a swell, you see. We beat a school 13-0 yesterday. I was in the team. I am going to try for a schol. at Marlborough soon. Goodbye. Congrats again.'

16 December. Weekend at College. Holy Communion in School Chapel. Wore my Medal Ribbon on my scarf for the first time. Preached on 'The Great Adventure'. Instead of School Prep at 8 p.m. I went into the big schoolroom and gave the boys an account of the Battle for the Passchendaele Ridge. Showed them some of the souvenirs which I have brought home. The most interesting of these are a German soldier's horse-hide pack, a half-exploded shrapnel shell with half of the shrapnel still in it, and the granite capital of a small pillar from the Cloth Hall at Ypres. Went round Whidborne Dormitory when the boys were going to bed.

17 December. Gave the Juniors a talk this morning and got them a half-holiday on the strength of my M.C. As it was too cold for footer they went for a walk and I went with them. After tea with Head's wife who was entertaining the Choir Trebles and wanted me to help amuse them. We played all sorts of games until it was time for them to go to bed. Went round Hanbury Dormitory this evening.

19 December. Investiture at Buckingham Palace—on 7th Anniversary of my Ordination in Canterbury Cathedral. 150 recipients of the M.C., including 2 other Chaplains. King shook hands after pinning on Cross. In my case he said 'I have much pleasure in giving you the Military Cross for distinguished Service.' . . . Mother in front of crowd at gate. She took hold of my arm and walked me off as though she was the most important person in London at the moment!

Tanner was home on extended leave, due to a severe attack of sciatica, and it was not until the end of February 1918 that he was passed fit. In a 'post-war reflection' he indicates that he was in no hurry to revert to the status of school chaplain:

Though for family reasons I naturally enjoyed the brief respite from the strain of war conditions which a leave in 'Blighty' gave me, I was invariably anxious and even eager to get back to the Battalion. It was the feeling that 'over there' life was a big thing which unsettled me at home and made me long to get back to the Battalion. In spite of the discomforts and dangers, life there was free from many of the pettinesses which so often mar ordinary daily life.

Tanner rejoined his Battalion shortly before the Germans launched their final offensive. His diary entry for 13 April records 'one of the most thrilling days of my existence'—a day that began with an orderly running down to the Battalion HQ in a cellar among the ruins of Neuve Eglise to announce 'The enemy are in the village, Sir, and are coming up from three directions.'

Tanner's lengthy account of the ding-dong battle that ensued, during which, but for the gallant action of the Adjutant (later awarded the V.C.) the Battalion would almost certainly have been cut off and forced to surrender, is the most gripping section of the diary. But only one episode has a bearing on his functions as a padre—this time, ironically, in the service of 'the Boche'. It relates to an occasion during the defence of the village when Tanner, who had been carrying ammunition for a Lewis gunner, was sprinting for cover as a German machine-gun opened fire.

. . . On going round the corner I saw the most horrible sight. The lane—a narrow leafy one with a high hedge on both sides—was absolutely littered with dead and dying Germans. They had evidently been trapped in their flight by our men and mown down.

As soon as I made my appearance it became obvious that they were not all dead, for I was greeted with moans and cries of 'Kamerad'. On going towards them I found

that five were still living. The poor wretches were terrified, quite expecting that I was going to shoot them. Two
were beyond all hope. One of them, who was lying in the
ditch at the right of the road, had had his stomach torn
open. He was just breathing but that was all and I could
do nothing more than offer a prayer for him as I passed on
to the others and gave them some water from their own
bottles. They seemed greatly surprised and relieved.

While doing this a bullet whizzed over my head and
then another, and I quickly realised that some German
sniper had spotted me moving about the lane and was
trying his luck. I lay down flat on the ground and peered
over the bank in his direction but could see nothing.
Presently some of our men came up by the end of the
lane. I told them where I thought the Boche was and they
went in his direction and evidently got him on the run
again as no more shots were fired across the lane. I then
returned to the village for stretcher-bearers and we
brought the three wounded Germans back to the Aid
Post.

Tanner, who himself led one party to safety when the
village was eventually evacuated, and who was later slightly
wounded in the leg by a shell splinter, was awarded a Bar to
the M.C. He quotes the Brigadier as saying, 'I'm disgusted
that it wasn't something better.'

During the last seven months of the war the Battalion was
frequently under fire, and burial services and the writing of
letters of condolence (accompanied by a personally inscribed
Memorial Card with the message 'Death is but the veil
through which men pass into a new, a richer and a fuller life')
became a regular part of his padre's duties. He records that he
is well satisfied with attendances at his voluntary services.
Though stating that he 'cannot understand the feelings of
those who have no time for religion', one entry suggests that

he was no longer as shocked as he had once been by the 'openly anti-religious':

> Had a long but entirely friendly argument with Farley, the new R.S.M., this evening. He says that the presence of suffering has made him an atheist and added quite frankly, 'There are two classes of people I hate—Padres and Policemen!' It was refreshing to get such frankness. He also said that there was no such thing as 'spiritual welfare'. In spite of this we get on very well together.

Right to the end Tanner's concern for the Battalion's spiritual welfare found public expression in the same tired old bromides. Here is a typically predictable extract from the last of his sermons to have been preserved, delivered two months before the end of the war:

> We're out here to do a certain job—a difficult job—and it's still unfinished and we, as England's sons, are charged to see it through. To falter or give way to war weariness at this stage would be to betray our trust. A cancer is eating out the heart of Europe, and it's got to be cut out and we have to take our share in doing it, or else our pals will have died in vain and our children will have to endure a war even bloodier than this one.
>
> Not only England but the whole civilised world is watching us, yes, and depending on us. So let's get to work again with renewed vigour and determination and do our bit and do it well, for the sake of the Regiment, for the sake of our homes, and of the boys and girls growing up in them, and, last but by no means least, for the honour of God and the triumph of right . . .

Tanner's most bizarre adventure occurred only two weeks before the end of the war, with the demoralised German army everywhere in retreat. He describes it as 'the experience of my life', and one can imagine that it would have rated high in the repertoire of war stories with which he would shortly be regaling the boys.of Weymouth College.

The 2nd Worcesters had crossed the river Selle and reached the outskirts of a village called Engelfontaine, the rest of it still occupied by the enemy. In the early hours of 26 October the Germans sent over a barrage of shells. After it had subsided Tanner, armed with a torch, set off to see if there were any wounded to be brought in.

. . . After going over the next cross-roads I passed, without realising it at the time, into that part of the village which was still in Boche hands. Suddenly, when passing the open door of a house, I became aware of someone standing just inside the doorway. I had hardly said 'Are you Worcesters?' when I discovered that they were two armed Germans.

At first I hardly knew what to do, but quickly pointed my torch at them—it was all I had—and said 'Hands up!' Evidently thinking that I was armed, and not being able to see in the darkness whether I was alone or not, they dropped their rifles and put their hands above their heads. Seeing light in the house, I went into the back room and found it unoccupied. Then, hearing cries in the cellar, I went down a few steps and saw that it was full of Boche, so I again pointed the torch at them, concealing its length as best I could in my sleeve, and called on them to surrender.

To my amazement no less than 22 of them came up the cellar steps holding up their hands and shouting 'Mercy, mercy, Kamerad!' The whole situation was so ridiculous that I could not help laughing to myself! I ordered the whole lot into the street and formed my captives into fours, went through them to ensure that they had no weapons, and then marched them down through the village to our Battalion HQ. One young chap, who could speak a bit of broken English, said 'Is it permitted for me to go and get my trousers?' but, under the circumstances, I was taking no risks and I said 'Nacht'. He then told me that there were more Germans in a house close by and wanted me to go with him and bring them out, but, being single-handed, I thought 'A bird in the hand is worth two in the bush' and decided to hold on to my twenty-four!

Some of the men of our 'A' Company, who were occupying the mine crater at the cross-roads, were highly amused as my little cavalcade of prisoners came towards them. The incident also caused no little amusement at BHQ and was soon sent over the phone to the Brigadier! There were a lot of stretcher cases at our Aid Post and we made use of my 24 prisoners to carry them down the Line.

Modestly Tanner later added a footnote: 'There is no doubt that the Germans' readiness to surrender was due to the fact that they regarded the War as lost as far as they were concerned and had become demoralised.'

The last diary entry is dated 25 March 1920, by which time Tanner had settled down again to the duties of Chaplain and Scoutmaster at Weymouth College, to which were now added the responsibilities of Junior School housemaster. It was a proud day for the school, as for him.

I was invested with a Bar to my M.C. by the King at Buckingham Palace. It was a much bigger affair than when I received my M.C. in 1917. It was held this time in one of the State Rooms. There was a large number of recipients of decorations and a correspondingly large number of relatives and friends. My Mother was again with me. A Military Band was playing during the proceedings.

It was with his mother that, in the following year, Tanner made a tour of the old battlefields: a last, lingering farewell to all that had been meant by 'over there', where life was 'a big thing'. The desolate landscapes were much as he remembered them—though landscapes now without figures.

A place of special pilgrimage was the German pillbox in the Ypres Salient, where he had spent those 72 hours under almost constant shellfire and the threat of a German counterattack. In Tanner's brief record of this part of the tour, accompanying the many snapshots he took, there is one revealing passage that suggests that, subconsciously at least, his belief in a divine dispensation had not altogether relieved him of 'all sense of anxiety and fear'.

In their hotel that night his mother was woken by sounds coming from his room. Her son was in the throes of a nightmare. In a strangled cry she heard the words, 'They've broken through! They've broken through!'

After Tanner's death in 1977, *The O.W. Budget*, journal of the Old Weymouthians' Club, devoted much of its space to 'appreciations of the life and work of our beloved "Priest"'. The glowing portrait of a 'Mr Chips' that emerges is one that could scarcely be expected from the phlegmatic pages of the war diary. Former masters and boys are unanimous in praise of his heartwarming qualities. The headmaster of Dean Close School, Cheltenham, where Tanner spent eleven years as chaplain and housemaster after the closure of Weymouth College in 1939, goes so far as to describe him as 'probably the greatest schoolmaster of this century'.

At the outbreak of the Second World War Tanner had again offered his services to the War Office as an army chaplain, but was unable to persuade them that, at 54, he was not too old to return to the field. So it was that his three years as a padre on the Western Front remained his only venture away from the tradition-bound ambience of the public school.

There is little mention in the journal of tributes to Tanner's functions as school chaplain. A former pupil recalls that he was 'not very impressive as a preacher—his religious and moral attitudes to life came over much more persuasively outside the chapel'. It is in his role as housemaster, and in his close identification with every school activity, that he is best remembered. Two extracts (the first written by an Old Weymouthian, the second by an old boy of Dean Close School) project his 'den' as a focal point of boarding school life, the most comforting of retreats for all and sundry.

. . . His study was open to all. We shall always retain a clear picture of the colossal coal fire, of boys sitting in the window seats heads bent over illustrated papers; of the rows of loose-leaf notebooks around the walls, the numerous volumes on all subjects which he found time to read, despite his multifarious activities, and of the mantelpiece adorned with all sorts of pictures and photographs and several caricatures of himself. It was the room of a man who preferred the comfort of others to the comfort of himself, which was only a facet of the cheery generosity which characterised all his actions. Not only his room was imprinted with his personality; the whole School bore its imprint. 'Priest' made his presence felt in any place . . .

. . . His hospitality was famous, and if at any time a visitor was found wandering uncertainly in the maze of corridors and stairs which led to his study, there was no need to ask whom he was seeking. Some strangers found their way to the right door simply by listening for the indescribable but characteristic laugh which was sure to be heard sooner or later. Within the study probably would be found half-a-dozen boys among the ruins of a substantial tea. At other times there would be coffee cups and a saucepan of milk on the gas-ring, invariably and inevitably boiling over while the attention of the host was otherwise engaged, probably in showing his latest batch of photographic prints ('This really is the only lead font in the whole county'). Occasionally the cheerful noise continued so long that the Headmaster in his study below would complain that he found it impossible to work. But it was difficult to be annoyed with Mr Tanner for long, and quite out of the question to quarrel with him . . .

For the last 25 years of his life, following his retirement in 1951, Tanner's life continued to revolve around his two old schools. Largely instrumental in reviving the Old Weymouthians' Club, he officiated at an annual Commemoration Service at the village church of nearby Radipole, where are preserved the school's 1914–18 memorials. His home at Preston near Weymouth (where in old age he was cared for by a housekeeper) was a Mecca for old boys of both schools, who were surprised and flattered to discover how much Tanner could recall of their boyhood exploits. Wrote one in *The O.W. Budget*:

> . . . On arrival one simply went through the open front door and made for the study in which he spent most of the day seated by the window overlooking his garden. It was a room crowded with furniture—cabinets containing his collection of stamps and many albums of photographs, crammed bookcases with a permanent overspill on chairs and tables, framed photographs on the walls and wherever else there was space available—the souvenirs of a lifetime. Always there was the same warm welcome, an eager demand for personal news, and a lively account of some recent event in which he had been involved. Time passed too quickly.

It was amongst this clutter of a lifetime that, some 12 years before his death, Tanner came across his war diaries and began to live again those battles long ago when life had seemed a 'big thing' and death a veil through which he might at any time pass. He began to correspond with some of the surviving members of his regiment. Among the mass of material he eventually donated to the Imperial War Museum (including the original mud-stained notebooks he had carried in the breast pocket of his tunic) is a letter from Sir Henry Morris-Jones, M.C.—the 'Doc' of the diary. At the age of 80, he looks back on the experiences they had shared in that pillbox charnel house near Passchendaele:

You certainly went through it in the First War and your Bar is a great honour. It was truly a horrible war. How we came alive out of the holocaust on the Menin Road I do not know. The journey up the line with those dozens of our poor Tommies lying prone, mutilated and dead was a pitiful sight. It is a marvel what the human body and soul can stand . . .

In Tanner's diary there is little indication that he was deeply affected by the 'pity of war', or that its horrors in any way caused him to rethink the simple credo of the school chapel. He returned to the cloistered security of a public school much as he had left, and for the rest of his life the winds of change passed him by. A friend recalls that, in looking back on his time as a padre, he expressed himself as well satisfied with what he had achieved. He was particularly gratified in rereading the replies of next-of-kin to the letters of condolence he had written—like that of one Tommy's mother which begins, 'I'm so glad to know that my Boy was buried comfortable . . .'

For his own funeral, conducted in the village church at Preston, near Weymouth, during the Easter week of 1977, Tanner had long before planned the Order of Service. As an expression of his views on life and death, it might well have accompanied that 'farewell' letter he had written to his mother from the Ypres Salient nearly 60 years before. The comforting belief he had so often passed on to the Tommies, that one's 'earthly task' had been planned out by God and that 'my times are in His hands' was finally echoed in his choice of the last hymn, sung by a packed congregation of old boys and masters: 'The day thou gavest, Lord, is ended'.

It was left to Tanner's old Dean Close School headmaster, writing in the Old Weymouthians' journal, to add an epitaph as confident as the one he had once pronounced on the long-forgotten victims of Passchendaele: 'There would be no trouble for him at St. Peter's Gate.'

CHAPTER SIX

SAINTLY
FATHER DOYLE

WHILE ACTING AS military chaplain during the Great War, there was in Father Willie Doyle's whole manner of life something so spiritual that it impressed all who met him. A few days before his death the Adjutant of the 9th Dublin Fusiliers, a Protestant, speaking of him to me, said: 'What is it makes Father Doyle so different from the rest of you priests? You R.C. Padres are streets above our fellows, but Father Doyle is as far above the rest of you as you are above them.'

It was thus that a Father Francis Browne wrote after the war about the fellow padre, killed during the Third Battle of Ypres in 1917, who had been recommended by his Divisional General for a posthumous V.C. but who himself scorned any earthly glory. A year before, during the Battle of the Somme, Doyle had written to his father: 'They have given me the M.C., but His crosses are far more welcome. I am sorry these rewards are given to chaplains, for surely he would be a poor specimen of the Lord's Anointed who would do his work for such a thing.'

Doyle, an Irish Jesuit, was remarkable not so much for what he did as for what he was. Outwardly he appeared a lively and endearing character, with a keen sense of humour. Only his intimates were aware of the spiritual aspirations that lay behind all his actions. From boyhood his consuming ambition had been to attain to a state of sainthood and to die a martyr's death. As a priest he had dedicated himself to a life of 'privation, suffering and sacrifice, accepted lovingly for the love of Jesus'. A discipline that went far beyond mere self-denial, he privately subjected himself to agonising penances reminiscent of the flagellant monks of medieval times. And for him the horrors of trench warfare were but another cross to be joyfully borne—and this time shared. He wrote to his father from the trenches in November 1916:

> I wonder if there is a happier man in France than I am. Just now Jesus is giving me great joy in tribulation, though conditions of living are about as uncomfortable as even S. Teresa could wish—perpetual rain, oceans of mud, damp, cold and a plague of rats. Yet I feel all this is a preparation for the future and that God is labouring in my soul for ends I do not clearly see as yet. Sometimes I kneel down with outstretched arms and pray God, if it is part of His divine plan, to rain down fresh privations and suffering . . .

To General Hickie, Commander-in-Chief of the 16th Division, in which Doyle served for 19 months up to his death, he was simply 'one of the bravest men who have fought or served out here'. In a letter to a friend after Doyle's death he wrote: 'He did his duty, and more than his duty, most nobly, and has left a memory and a name behind him that will never be forgotten.'

In Catholic circles at least, that memory was kept alive for a decade or so after the war. A lengthy biography, the bulk of it dealing with his life before becoming a padre, was published in 1920, reprinted five times and translated into six languages (including German). But it has been long out of print, and this chapter, largely based on the letters Doyle wrote from the front, will come as a revelation to most readers. Rarely can a padre have attained so nearly to saintliness, and at the same time come so close to the hearts of the Tommies he served.

Some 25 per cent of padres at the front were Catholic (by the end of the war 649 out of 3,475). That they were much more readily accepted by the Tommy (whatever his beliefs) than their Anglican opposite numbers is understandable. Most of them came from working-class backgrounds (Doyle was an exception), and there were none of the barriers that separated the average Tommy from the most well-meaning of public-school-orientated Anglicans. And, unlike most of their opposite numbers, Catholic padres were respected as spending much of their time in the line, sharing the same risks and hardships as the fighting troops. Only there could they fully carry out their duties as priests, in the administration of the Sacraments. Even to the non-Catholic, to whom the Mass, confessions and absolutions were meaningless rituals, there was something commendably professional about the Catholic padre. The average Anglican, by comparison, seemed an amateur.

First-hand accounts by Catholic padres are a rarity. And in reading Doyle's letters one is immediately struck how different were the functions of Catholic and Protestant padres. The whole emphasis is less on morale-boosting than on the saving of souls. There are few mentions of church parades, of camp recreations and entertainments, even of life in the officers' mess. War aims, or the justice of the Allied cause, are not his concern. To him the Germans are not 'the Boche' or 'the Hun' but 'brother Fritz', and he shows almost as much concern for wounded enemy prisoners as for his own men. After one batch of Germans has been brought in, he writes:

I must confess my heart goes out to these unfortunate soldiers whose sufferings have been terrific. I can't share the general sentiment that 'they deserve what they get

and one better.' For after all are they not children of the
same loving Saviour who said: 'Whatever you do to one
of these my least ones you do it for Me.' I try to show any
little kindness I can . . .

That Doyle appeared to regard the war as a divine judgement on a sinful world is suggested by his comments on a
crucifix he found hanging on the wall of an otherwise ruined
village church:

The eyes are open, gazing as it were upon the scene of
desolation, and though the wall upon which the Crucifix
hangs is riddled with bullet holes and shell splinters, the
image is untouched save for one round bullet hole just
through the heart. The whole thing may be only chance,
but it is a striking sight, and cannot fail to impress one and
bring home the fact that, if God is scourging the world as
it well deserves, He is not indifferent to the sorrows and
sufferings of His children.

Though for Doyle the Irish Catholic was the salt of the
earth, there was evidently nothing overtly sectarian in his
dealings with others. 'Father Doyle was beloved and respected, not only by those of his Faith, but equally by
Protestants, to which denomination I belong,' wrote an
army doctor who served with him. But in reading his letters,
so infused with a general concern for the sufferings of others,
one is disturbingly aware of the dichotomy that lay at the
heart of his faith.

Inescapable for him (as for any Catholic) was the belief that
humanity was divided into the sheep and the goats, that only
the faithful of the 'true Church' would go to Heaven (or, as
an intermediate state, to Purgatory), and that for the rest of
mankind Hell awaited. In preaching to the converted, Doyle
has no hesitation in making this tacitly clear, as indicated in
one of the outlines for sermons he jotted down in his notebook:

A serious word—matter of life and death, eternal life, the salvation or damnation of many depend on it. Going to the Front in a couple of weeks, in midst of shot and shell, in danger at any moment of instant death. Are you ready to face God: none of us is afraid, it has to come sometime, but, 'know ye not there is a Judgement?' I am pleading for your immortal souls; it matters little in the end whether we have been rich or poor, lives of hardship or pleasure, but to save one's soul or lose it matters much. It may be hard for some to square up accounts (not half as hard as you think) but a million times harder to burn in Hell, cursing your folly.

In a letter to the *Irish Catholic*, written under a pseudonym, in May 1917, Doyle goes so far as to solicit help in the saving of Catholic souls.

. . . With all the spiritual help now at their disposal, even in the very firing line, we may be fairly confident that few, if any, of our Catholic men are unprepared to meet Almighty God. That does not mean they are fit for Heaven. God's justice must be fully satisfied, and the debt of forgiven sin fully atoned for in Purgatory. Hence I venture to appeal to the great charity of your readers to provide 'comforts for our dead soldiers' by having Masses offered for their souls . . .

In his references to those beyond the pale, Doyle appears to dodge the issue. An instance is his description of some corpses he came across on the battlefield at Loos—corpses he could not have known to have been of Catholics 'prepared to meet Almighty God'. His bromides about 'sleeping in peace' and of being reunited in Heaven could be those of any Anglican padre, apart from a veiled hint that Purgatory might have been their initial destination.

. . . A large mound caught my eye. Four pairs of feet were sticking out, one a German, judging by his boots, and three Frenchmen—friend and foe are sleeping their long last sleep in peace together. They were decently covered compared with the next I saw; a handful of earth covered the wasted body, but the legs and arms and head were exposed to view. He seemed quite a young lad, with fair, almost golden, hair. 'An unknown soldier' was all the rough cross over him told me about him; but I thought of the sorrowing mother, far away, thinking of her boy who was 'missing', and hoping against hope that he might one day come back. Thank God, Heaven one day will reunite them both. I found a shovel near at hand, and after a couple of hours' stiff work was able to cover the bodies decently, so that on earth at least they might rest in peace.

There are discrepancies, too, between Doyle's avowed abhorrence of war ('If only the world, Allied and German, could see and hear what we see and hear daily, there would soon be a shout for peace at ANY price' he writes) and his unbounded admiration for the fighting qualities of the Irish. He can even see those qualities as a reflection of their religion. In one passage, after referring to the number of converts being made, both among officers and men, who have been 'immensely impressed by what the Catholic priests, alone of all the Chaplains at the front, are able to do for their men, both living and dying,' he writes:

It is an admitted fact that the Irish Catholic soldier is the bravest and best man in a fight, but few know that he draws his courage from the strong Faith with which he is filled and the help which comes from the exercises of his religion.

Doyle himself was a distinctive figure in the trenches in that he rarely wore a tin helmet or carried a gas respirator, unless directly ordered to do so by a superior officer. Heedless of danger, the courage so applauded by others (but which he himself put in quite a different perspective) was most frequently exhibited in the giving of absolutions to the dying. Time and again he risked his life, sometimes in no-man's-land, to speed a soul to heaven. He writes of a typical occasion:

> The Rites of the Church were quickly administered, though it was hard to find a sound spot on that poor smashed face for the Holy Oils, and my hands were covered with his blood. The moaning stopped. I pressed the crucifix to his lips and he murmured after me: 'My Jesus, mercy', and then, as I gave him the Last Blessing, his head fell back and the loving arms of Jesus were pressing to his Sacred Heart the soul of another of His friends . . .

What distinguishes Doyle's accounts of the battlefield, the emotive language apart, is his constant awareness of the presence of God. Far from being an abstraction, this could be a tangible presence. There is one description, during the Battle of Messines in 1917, that must read to a non-Christian as so much mumbo-jumbo, but which to Doyle was the reality at the heart of his faith: an occasion when God was not only at his side on the battlefield, but in his arms.

> . . . As I knew there was no chance of saying Mass at our temporary chapel, I had taken the precaution of bringing several Consecrated Particles with me, so that I should not be deprived of Holy Communion. It was the Feast of Corpus Christi and I thought of the many processions of the Blessed Sacrament which were being held at the moment all over the world. Surely there never was a

stranger one than mine that day, as I carried the God of Consolation over the blood-stained battlefield. There was no music to welcome Him save the scream of a passing shell; the flowers that strewed His path were the broken, bleeding bodies of those for whom He had once died; and the only Altar of Repose was the heart of one who was working for Him alone, striving in a feeble way to make Him some return for all His love and goodness . . .

A fellow priest described Doyle as having about him 'a charisma of sanctity that influences all who come in contact with him'. That this was in no way off-putting to the Tommy is clear from the numbers of tributes paid to him after his death, both by Protestant Ulstermen and Irish Catholics, which were summed up in a comment by a war correspondent: 'They remember him as a saint—they speak his name with tears.' The affection in which he was held is most tellingly indicated in a reference he himself makes (without undue immodesty) to an encounter with a burly Fusilier in a village near the front:

He was one of my old boys, and having had a couple of glasses of beer—'It wouldn't scratch the back of your throat, that French stuff'—was in the mood to be complimentary. 'We miss you sorely, Father, in the battalion,' he said, 'we do be always talking about you.' Then, in a tone of great confidence: 'Look, Father, there isn't a man who wouldn't give the whole of the world, if he had it, for your little toe! That's the truth.' The poor fellow meant well, but 'the stuff that wouldn't scratch his throat' certainly helped his imagination and eloquence.

Instances of Doyle's popularity with all manner of people abound in the 600 pages of Professor Alfred O'Rahilly's biography (*Father William Doyle, S.J.: A Spiritual Study*). But its publication in 1920 must have come as a scarcely credible revelation to almost everyone who thought they knew him. And a brief résumé of his early life is necessary to indicate what O'Rahilly calls 'the real man within, so hidden and unsuspected and, to most men, unintelligible'.

Born at Melrose, County Dublin, in 1873, son of an official of the High Court of Justice in Ireland and youngest of seven children, Doyle had an outwardly unremarkable middle-class upbringing. As a boy one of his favourite games was staging battles with model soldiers on the nursery floor with a brother—usually Irish against English. At a Catholic boarding school in England he was a general favourite with his school fellows, excelling at sports. No one suspected that from an early age he had made up his mind to be a saint and a martyr.

An early indication of his lifelong struggle for self-mastery and perfection was an occasion when, at the beginning of Lent, an aunt came across him gesticulating in front of a mirror and talking to his reflection: 'You villain, you wretch, I'll starve you, I'll murder you! Not a sweet will you get, not a bit of cake will you get!' His favourite childhood reading were the twelve volumes of Butler's Lives of the Saints. On one occasion the parents of some friends of his complained that their children had come home with their legs covered in stings following a game Willie had invented. Called 'The Penny Torture' it required the contestants, after depositing a penny each in a kitty, to march up and down in a field of nettles. It was Willie who had lasted out the longest and pocketed the kitty.

Professor O'Rahilly, who had known Doyle personally, was at pains throughout his book to make clear that there was nothing outwardly 'abnormal' about him, that his most noted characteristic was a sense of humour that tended towards practical jokes and 'harmless mischief', and that he kept closely to himself the spiritual conflict that raged so obsessively within him. That conflict, which would never have been known about had it not been for the discovery of his secret 'spiritual diaries' after his death, forms the bulk of the biography. It is here of interest only in explaining Doyle's attitude to the war as but the final stage of his self-imposed Via Dolorosa.

His pilgrimage could be said to have started when, as a novitiate aged 20, he penned a prayer to the Virgin Mary dedicating himself to a life of 'slow martyrdom by earnest hard work and constant self-denial'. Written in his own blood were the words: 'With my blood I promise thee to keep this resolution, do thou, sweet Mother, assist me and obtain for me the one favour I wish and long for: to die a Jesuit martyr. May God's will, not mine be done. Amen.'

'Other souls may travel by other roads, the road of pain is mine', was the conviction that later led Doyle to compose a long and chilling prayer to Jesus.

> . . . You want me to crucify myself in every way I can think of; never if possible to be without some pain or discomfort; to die to myself and to my love of ease and comfort—to crucify my body in every way I can think of, bearing heat, cold, little sufferings without relief, constantly, if possible, wearing some instrument of penance . . .

Even some Catholic reviewers of the biography were horrified by 'the recital of deeds which might have been regarded as relegated to ancient hagiographies', and in which the wearing of the traditional hair-shirt was a comparatively minor discomfort. These are among the penances Doyle subjected himself to, while staying in Jesuit religious houses or even when engaged in mission work in cities in Ireland, England and Scotland. They were confided in a letter to an intimate only because Doyle felt he had been divinely instructed to do so.

Several times I have undressed and rolled in furze bushes. The pain of the thousands of little pricks is intense for days afterwards.

I have a waist-chain of three links. I heated it at the fire (not red-hot of course) and put it round my body. That hurt and raised some nice blisters.

I have used the heavy chain as a discipline sometimes. It is severe, as it bruises the flesh, and the points are driven in and draw blood.

I set my alarm for three o'clock when it is freezing, slip out of the house in my night-shirt, and stand up to my neck in the pond, praying for sinners. I get in and out two or three times till petrified with cold.

Once I made a discipline with some razor-blades, I admit this was foolish as some blows cut to the very bone and the blood ran down till a small pool had formed on the floor . . .

The severest penance, which he somehow passed off as an 'accident' when forced to get medical attention, harks back to his childhood and gives some inkling as to the motivation:

That day the love of Jesus Christ was burning in my heart with the old longing to suffer much for Him and even to give my life in martyrdom. This thought was in my mind when, crossing a lonely field late that evening, I came across a forest of old nettles. Here was a chance! Had not the Saints suffered in this way for Him with joy and gladness of heart? I undressed and walked up and down until my whole body was one big blister, smarting and stinging. Words could never describe the sweet but horrible agony from that moment till far into the next day. Not for a moment did I close my eyes, for as the poison worked into the blood the fever mounted and the pain increased . . .

In a footnote (the one occasion in the biography when sex is directly alluded to) O'Rahilly mentions instances of Saint Benedict throwing himself naked into nettles and briars 'to overcome a temptation of the flesh'. But celibacy, he indicates, was no problem for Doyle. He quotes him as writing in a letter that 'until I began my theology at thirty-one I was quite ignorant of most sexual matters'. A colleague, he adds, had confirmed that Doyle 'found it hard to realise the difficulties of those struggling with impurity and the awful fascination of the sin, just as those who have never taken strong drink fail to appreciate the difficulties and temptations of the drunkard.' It is noticeable, indeed, that, as a padre, Doyle makes only one direct reference to the temptations of the flesh. In one of his outlines for a sermon he has jotted down: 'Avoid devil (women).'

Doyle offered his services as a chaplain shortly after war was declared. For him it was a God-sent alternative to the foreign mission field (preferably a leper colony in the Congo) he had hankered for, but been denied. On his eventual appointment to the 16th Irish Division, in November 1915, he wrote to a friend: 'My heart is full of gratitude to Jesus for giving me this chance of being really generous and of leading a life that will be truly crucified.' He had a premonition that he would be killed—and the strangest of reasons for not wanting to die: 'It is not that I am afraid of death, but the thought that I could never again do more for God or suffer for Him in heaven makes the sacrifice too bitter for words.'

As late as 1915, shortly before his appointment, Doyle was still subjecting himself to what his biographer calls his 'holy follies', as some notebook extracts indicate: 'Severe discipline with thorns. Slept on floor. No fire. Got into pond at two. Hair-shirt six hours. Wore waist-chain during motor drive. Discipline with razor. Hung on cross. Walked barefoot on stones. Ditto on nettles.'

It is to be supposed that such refinements of suffering

became unnecessary on the Western Front. But as gruelling in a mental way was the ceaseless discipline of prayer and the telling of beads to which he continued to devote every idle moment. To these, even in the trenches, he added 'nocturnal adoration before the Blessed Sacraments'. 'Last night I prayed in my dugout at Kemmel from 9 till 5 (eight hours), most of the time on my knees,' he wrote in October 1916. 'I bound myself beforehand by vow in order not to let myself off. Though I had only two hours sleep, I am not very tired or weary today. Jesus wants more of these nights of prayer, adoration and atonement.'

Though the officers censoring his letters to his widowed father must have read with some surprise the frequent passages recording his spiritual travails and ecstasies, little of the ascetic or mystic was apparent to the men he served. A reference to him dining in the officers' mess pictures him as 'full of chat and banter', though eating and drinking noticeably less than anybody else. To the Tommies he was always 'little Father Doyle'—the 'little' being purely a term of endearment (he was 5ft 10in tall).

How Doyle would have fared in an English regiment is a matter for conjecture. As it was, he was in his element in the Irish regiments he served—the 8th Royal Irish Fusiliers and the Royal Inniskilling Fusiliers from February to December 1916, thereafter the 9th Royal Dublin Fusiliers and the 6/7th Royal Irish Rifles. 'Our poor lads are just grand', he writes in an early letter from the Loos front. 'They curse like troopers all the day, they give the Germans Hell, Purgatory and Heaven all combined at night, and next morning come kneeling in the mud for Mass and Holy Communion when they get the chance; and they beam all over with genuine pleasure when their padre comes past their dugout or meets them in the trenches.'

Had Doyle been pressed to ascribe any favouritism to the Almighty, he must have come down on the side of 'brave

Paddy from the Green Island'. The Irish patriot in him not
infrequently seems to get the better of the committed man of
God. 'They have all the dash and go of the hot-blooded Celtic
race', he writes of the Irish Fusiliers during the Battle of the
Somme. He even records without disapproval an engagement in which they took it upon themselves to fire on
English troops who had panicked and fled from a German
strongpoint before continuing their own assault. And politics openly rears its head in a report by a fellow padre of a
sermon Doyle preached at St Omer Cathedral shortly before
the Third Battle of Ypres to a congregation of 2,500 mostly
Catholic Irish.

. . . He spoke wonderfully of the coming of the Old Irish
Brigade in their wanderings over the Low Countries. It
was here that he touched daringly, but ever so cleverly,
on Ireland's part in the war. Fighting for Ireland and not
fighting for Ireland, or rather fighting for Ireland
through another . . .

In a footnote O'Rahilly comments:

It certainly required some diplomatic skill to appeal to
Irish regiments in the British Army by evoking memories of the Irish Brigade which had fought against the
English in Flanders three hundred years before. Nor was
it easy, without hurting English susceptibilities, to con-
vey the fact that Irish soldiers who were listening were
fighting for what they believed was Ireland's cause as
well as Belgium's.

The final section of the biography dealing with Doyle's 19
months as a padre amounts to some 80,000 words, and it is
here possible only to give extracts from his descriptions, in
letters to his father, of the three major engagements in which
he participated—the Somme, Messines and Ypres.

It was two months after the launching of the Allied offen-

sive that the 16th Division was moved south from the Loos
sector to the Somme. On 5 September 1916 the 8th Royal
Irish Fusiliers were ordered to advance and hold the front line
at Leuze Wood, already the scene of much desperate fighting.
Doyle accompanied them:

The first part of our journey lay through a narrow trench,
the floor of which consisted of deep thick mud, and the
bodies of dead men trodden underfoot. It was horrible
beyond description, but there was no help for it, and
on the half-rotten corpses of our own brave men we
marched in silence, everyone busy with his own
thoughts. I shall spare you gruesome details, but you can
picture one's sensations as one felt the ground yield under
one's foot, and one sank down through the body of some
poor fellow.

Half an hour of this and out on the open into the middle
of the battlefield of some days previous. The wounded, at
least I hope so, had all been removed, but the dead lay
there stiff and stark, with open staring eyes, just as they
had fallen. Good God, such a sight! I had tried to prepare
myself for this, but all I had read or pictured gave me little
idea of the reality. Some lay as if they were sleeping
quietly, others had died in agony, while the whole
ground, every foot of it, was littered with heads or limbs,
or pieces of torn human bodies. In the bottom of one hole
lay a British and a German soldier, locked in a deadly
embrace, neither had any weapon, but they had fought
on to the bitter end. Another couple seemed to have
realised that the horrible struggle was none of their
making, and that they were both children of the same
God; they had died hand-in-hand praying for and for-
giving one another. A third face caught my eye, a tall,
strikingly handsome young German, not more, I should
say, than eighteen. He lay there calm and peaceful, with a

smile of happiness on his face, as if he had a glimpse of Heaven before he died. Ah, if only his poor mother could have seen her boy it would have soothed the pain of her broken heart.

We pushed on rapidly through that charnel house, for the stench was fearful, till we stumbled across a sunken road. Here the retreating Germans had evidently made a last desperate stand, but had been caught by our artillery fire. The dead lay in piles, the blue uniforms broken by many a khaki-clad body. I saw the ruins of what was evidently the dressing station, judging by the number of bandaged men about; but a shell had found them out even here and swept them all into the net of death.

A halt for a few minutes gave me the opportunity I was waiting for. I hurried along from group to group, and as I did the men fell on their knees to receive absolution. A few words to give them courage, for no man knew if he would return alive. A 'God bless and protect you, boys,' and I passed on to the next company. As I did, a soldier stepped out of the ranks, caught me by the hand, and said: 'I am not a Catholic, sir, but I want to thank you for that beautiful prayer.' The regiments moved on to the wood, while the doctor and I took up our position in the dressing room to wait for the wounded. This was a dugout on the hill facing Leuze Wood, and had been in German occupation the previous afternoon.

To give you an idea of my position. From where I stood the ground sloped down steeply into a narrow valley, while on the opposite hill lay the wood, half of which the Fusiliers were now holding, the Germans occupying the rest; the distance across being so short I could easily follow the movements of our men without a glass.

Fighting was going on all round, so that I was kept busy, but all the time my thoughts and my heart were with my poor boys in the wood opposite. They had reached it safely, but the Germans had somehow worked round the sides and temporarily cut them off. No food or water could be sent up, while ten slightly wounded men who tried to come back were shot down, one after another. To make matters worse, our own artillery began to shell them, inflicting heavy losses, and though repeated messages were sent back, continued doing so for a long time. It appears the guns had fired so much that they were becoming worn out, making the shells fall 300 yards short.

Under these circumstances it would be madness to try and reach the wood, but my heart bled for the wounded and dying lying there alone. When dusk came I made up my mind to try and creep through the valley, more especially as the fire had slackened very much. As I was setting out I met a sergeant who argued the point with me. 'You can do little good, Father,' he said, 'down there in the wood, and will only run a great risk. Wait till night comes and then we shall be able to bring all the wounded up here. Don't forget that, though we have plenty of officers, we have only one priest to look after us.' The poor fellow was so much in earnest I decided to wait a little at least.

It was well I did so, for shortly afterwards the Germans opened up a terrific bombardment and launched a counter-attack on the wood. Some of the Cornwalls, who were holding a corner of the wood, broke and ran, jumping right on top of the Fusiliers. Brave Paddy from the Green Isle stood his ground and rose to the occasion, first shooting the men from Cornwall, and then hunted the Germans with cold steel.

Meanwhile we on the opposite hill were having a most unpleasant time. A wounded man had reported that the enemy had captured the wood. Communication was broken and Headquarters had no information of what was going on. At that moment an orderly dashed in with the startling news that the Germans were in the valley, and actually climbing our hill. Jerusalem! We non-combatants might easily escape to the rear, but who would protect the wounded? They could not be abandoned. If it were daylight the Red Cross might give us protection, but in the darkness of the night the enemy would not think twice about flinging a dozen bombs down the steps of the dugout. I looked round at the blood-stained walls and shivered. A nice coward, am I not? Thank God the situation was not quite so bad as reported; our men got the upper hand and drove back the attack, but that half-hour of suspense will live long in my memory.

Doyle's letter, written some days after the event, ends there. His next describes the Irish regiments' storming of the village of Ginchy, a German stronghold which English troops had earlier failed to capture, on 9 September. Because the 8th Fusiliers had lost so many officers, they were held in reserve.

. . . Shortly before 5 p.m. I went up to the hill in front of the village, and was just in time to see our men leap from their trenches and dart up the slope, only to be met by a storm of bullets from concealed machine-guns. It was my first real view of a battle at close quarters, an experience not easily forgotten. Almost simultaneously all our guns, big and little, opened a terrific barrage behind the village, to prevent the enemy bringing up reinforcements, and in half a minute the scene was hidden by the smoke of thousands of bursting shells, British and German.

The wild rush of our Irish lads swept the Germans away like chaff. The first line went clean through the village and out the other side, and were it not for the officers, acting under orders, would certainly be in Berlin by this time! Meanwhile the supports had cleared the cellars and dugouts of their defenders; the town was ours and all was well. At the same time a feeling of uneasiness was about. Rumour said some other part of the line had failed to advance, the Germans were breaking through, etc. One thing was certain, the guns had not ceased.

About nine o'clock the Fusiliers were getting ready to be relieved by another regiment when there came an urgent order to hurry up to the Front. To my dying day I shall never forget that half-hour, as we pushed across the open, our only light the flash of bursting shells, tripping over barbed wire, stumbling and walking on the dead, expecting every moment to be blown into Eternity. We were halted in a trench at the rear of the village, and there till four in the morning we lay on the ground listening to the roar of the guns and the scream of the shells flying overhead, not knowing if the next moment might not be our last. Fortunately, we were not called upon to attack, and our casualties were very light. But probably because the terrible strain of the past week was beginning to tell, or the Lord wished to give me a little merit by suffering more, the agony and fear and suspense of those six hours seemed to surpass the whole of the seven days.

We were relieved on Sunday morning, 10th, at four o'clock, and crawled back (I can use no other word) to the camp in the rear. My feet, perhaps, are the most painful of all, as we were not allowed to remove our boots even at night. But otherwise I am really well, thank God, and a few days' good rest will make me better than ever. At present we march one day and rest the next, but I do not know where.

For his bravery in these engagements Doyle was awarded the M.C. And that he was prepared to risk his life for the dead, as much as for the living and the dying, is apparent from a subsequent letter, in which he recalls a Mass for the Dead he celebrated one morning.

. . . By cutting a piece out of the side of the trench, I was just able to stand in front of my tiny altar, a biscuit box supported on two German bayonets. God's angels, no doubt, were hovering overhead, but so were the shells, hundreds of them, and I was a little afraid that when the earth shook with the crash of the guns, the chalice might be overturned.

Round about me on every side was the biggest congregation I ever had: behind the altar, on either side and in front, row after row, sometimes crowding one upon the other, but all quiet and silent, as if they were straining their ears to catch every syllable of that tremendous act of Sacrifice—but every man was dead! Some had lain there for a week and were foul and horrible to look at, with faces black and green. Others had only just fallen, and seemed rather sleeping than dead, but there they lay, for none had time to bury them, brave fellows every one, friend and foe alike, while I held in my unworthy hands the God of Battles, their Creator and their Judge, and prayed Him to give rest to their souls. Surely that Mass for the Dead, in the midst of, and surrounded by the dead, was an experience not easily to be forgotten.

Nine months later, from the Ypres Salient, Doyle writes:

We are on the eve of a tremendous battle and the danger will be very great. Sometimes I think God wishes the actual sacrifice of my life—the offering of it was made long ago. But if so, that almost useless life will be given most joyfully. I feel wonderful peace and confidence in leaving myself absolutely in God's Hands. Only I know it would not be right, I would like never to take shelter from bursting shells; and up to a few days ago, till ordered by the Colonel, I never wore a steel helmet . . .

With or without a helmet, Doyle survived the Battle of Messines, heralded by a week-long artillery bombardment and culminating, on 7 June 1917, in the most shattering explosion of the war, when seventeen mines were exploded under the German positions. At 1 a.m. that morning Doyle and Father Browne, who had now joined him, held a private Mass in their little sandbagged chapel near the line and served the Sacraments to each other. At 2.30 a.m. they put on their battle kit and made for their respective aid posts.

. . . It wanted half an hour to zero time. The guns had ceased firing; for a moment at least there was peace on earth and a calm which was almost more trying than the previous roar to us who knew what was coming. I pictured to myself our men, row upon row waiting in the darkness for the word to charge, and on the other side the Germans in their trenches and dugouts, little thinking that seventeen huge mines were laid under their feet, needing only a spark to blow them into eternity. The tension of waiting was terrific, the strain almost unbearable. One felt inclined to scream out and send them warning. But all I could do was to stand on top of the trench and give them Absolution, trusting to God's mercy to speed it so far.

Even now I can scarcely think of the scene which followed without trembling with horror. Punctually to the second at 3.10 a.m. there was a deep muffled roar; the ground in front of where I stood rose up, as if some giant had wakened from his sleep and was bursting his way through the earth's crust, and then I saw seventeen huge columns of smoke and flames shoot hundreds of feet into the air, while masses of clay and stones, tons in weight, were hurled about like pebbles. I never before realised what an earthquake was like, for not only did the ground quiver and shake, but actually rocked backwards and forwards, so that I kept on my feet with difficulty.

Before the debris of the mines had begun to fall to earth, the 'wild Irish' were over the top of the trenches and on the enemy, though it seemed certain they must be killed to a man by the falling avalanche of clay. Even a stolid English Colonel standing near was moved to enthusiasm: 'My God!' he said, 'what soldiers! They fear neither man nor devil!' Why should they? They had made their peace with God. He had given them His own Sacred Body to eat that morning, and they were going now to face death, as only Irish Catholic lads can do, confident of victory and cheered by the thought that the reward of Heaven was theirs. Nothing could stop such a rush, and so fast was the advance that the leading files actually ran into the barrage of our guns, and had to retire.

Meanwhile hell itself seemed to have been let loose. With the roar of the mines came the deafening crash of our guns, hundreds of them. How the Germans were able to put up the resistance they did was a marvel to everybody, for our shells fell like hailstones. In a few moments they took up the challenge and soon things on our side became warm and lively.

My men did not go over in the first wave, they were held in reserve to move up as soon as the first objective had been taken and resist any counter-attack. Most of them were waiting behind a thick sand-bag wall not far from the dressing station where I was, which enabled me to keep an eye on them.

The shells were coming over thick and fast now, and at last what I expected and feared happened. A big 'crump' hit the wall fair and square, blew three men into a field 50 yards away, and buried five others who were in a small dugout. For a moment I hesitated, for the horrible sight fairly knocked the 'starch' out of me and a couple more 'crumps' did not help to restore my courage.

I climbed out of the trench and ran across the open, as abject a coward as ever walked on two legs, till I reached the three dying men, and then the 'perfect trust' came back to me and I felt no fear. A few seconds sufficed to absolve and anoint my poor boys, and I jumped to my feet, only to go down on my face faster than I got up, as an express train from Berlin roared by.

The five men buried were calling for help, but the others standing around seemed paralysed with fear, all save one sergeant, whose language was worthy of the occasion and rose to a noble height of sublimity. He was working like a Trojan, tearing the sandbags aside, and welcomed my help with a mingled blessing and curse. The others joined in with pick and shovel, digging and pulling, till the sweat streamed from our faces, and the blood from our hands, but we got three of the buried men out alive, the other two had been killed by the explosion.

Once again I had evidence of the immense confidence our men have in their priest. It was quite evident that they were rapidly becoming demoralised, as the best of troops will who have to remain inactive under heavy shellfire. Little groups were running from place to place for greater shelter, and the officers seemed to have lost control. I walked along the line of men, crouching behind the sandbag wall, and was amused to see the ripple of smiles light up the terrified lads' faces (so many were mere boys) as I went by. By the time I got back again the men were laughing and chatting as if all danger was miles away, for quite unintentionally, I had given them courage by walking along without my gas mask or steel helmet, both of which I had forgotten in my hurry.

When the regiment moved forward, the Doctor and I went with it. By this time the 'impregnable' ridge was in our hands and the enemy retreating down the far side. I spent the rest of that memorable day wandering over the battlefield looking for the wounded, and had the happiness of helping many a poor chap, for shells were flying about on all sides . . .

Eight weeks later, on the eve of the Third Battle of Ypres, Doyle writes: ' "Success is certain" our Generals tell us, but I cannot help wondering what are the plans of the Great Leader, and what the result will be when He has issued His orders.' For him the 'call' was to come just two weeks later—unexpectedly. For by now his early presentiment of death had faded. His numerous 'miraculous escapes' had led him to believe that God had ordained his experiences at the front 'as a "novitiate" in preparation for my real life's work'. In his last letter to his father, written the day before he was killed, he wrote: 'My old armchair up in Heaven is not ready yet.'

The six days and seven nights Doyle spent continuously in the shell-torn morass of the Ypres battlefield were more fraught with danger, but less dramatically eventful, than those he had spent on the Somme. A new horror he encountered was the Germans' first use of mustard gas. Designed to disable rather than to kill, it raised blisters and burned men's bodies where the vapour was condensed into a reddish powder, blinded them for a week or more, and choked their lungs.

In reading his allusion to this latest refinement in the science of warfare, one cannot help wondering to what extent Doyle was inured to the idea of pain, as one who had long ago chosen the 'road of pain' as a means of salvation. Did he in any way equate those 'disciplines' to which he had for so long subjected himself with the immeasurably greater agonies of the battlefield? Though hair-shirts, waist-chains, nettles, razor blades, icy ponds, could scarcely be compared with impalement on barbed wire, mutilation by shell fragment or bayonet, searing by poison gas or slow drowning in a mud-filled crater, it is clear that he accepted suffering either as a chastisement from God or as a means of obtaining 'merit'. Physical agonies come secondarily for him to the state of a man's soul. And, at Ypres as elsewhere, the sufferings he witnessed appear to have strengthened rather than weakened his implicit belief in the living presence of God and His crucified Son.

God was certainly at the forefront of Doyle's mind as he marched with his regiments towards the sound of the guns as the offensive was launched:

It was 1.30 a.m. when our first halting place was reached, and as we march again at three, little time was wasted getting to sleep. It was the morning of July 31st, the Feast of St. Ignatius, a day dear to every Jesuit, but doubly so to the soldier sons of the soldier saint. Was it to be Mass or sleep? Nature said sleep, but grace won the day, and while the weary soldiers slumbered the Adorable Sacrifice was offered for them, that God would bless them in the coming fight and, if it were His Holy Will, bring them safely through it. Mass and thanksgiving over, a few precious moments of rest on the floor of a hut, and we have fallen into line once more.

As we do, the dark clouds are lit up with red and golden flashes of light, the earth quivers with the simultaneous crash of thousands of guns, and in imagination we can picture the miles of our trenches spring to life as the living stream of men pours over the top—the Third Battle of Ypres has begun.

Men's hearts beat faster, and nerves seem to stretch and vibrate like harp strings as we march steadily on ever nearer and nearer towards the raging fight, on past battery after battery of huge guns and howitzers belching forth shells which ten men could scarcely lift, on past the growing streams of motor ambulances, each with its sad burden of broken bodies, the first drops of that torrent of wounded which will pour along the road. I fancy not a few were wondering how long would it be till they were carried past in the same way, or was this the last march they would ever make till the final Roll Call on the Great Review Day? . . .

The Irish troops were being held in reserve for the opening stages of the battle, and it was not until five days later that Doyle reached the front. His accounts from now on were contained in two long letters he sent to his father shortly before he was killed, and are based on jottings he made in his notebook. The action for which Doyle was recommended for a posthumous V.C. occurred on the day he was killed, 16 August, the day when the Irish attacked *en masse* and were decimated. Up till then, as these final extracts will show, there had been little in the way of action, but Doyle was as tireless as ever in his ministrations.

5 August. All day I have been busy hearing the men's confessions, and giving batch after batch Holy Communion. A consolation surely to see them crowding to the Sacraments, but a sad one too, because I know for many of them it is the last Absolution they will ever receive, and the next time they meet our Blessed Lord will be when they see him face to face in Heaven.

As the men line up on Parade, I go from company to company giving a General Absolution which I know is a big comfort to them, and then I shoulder my pack. Though we are in fighting kit, there is no small load to carry: a haversack containing little necessary things, and three days' rations which consist of tinned corn beef, hard biscuits, tea and sugar; two full water-bottles; a couple of gas-helmets, the new one weighing nine pounds but guaranteed to keep out the smell of the Old Boy himself; then a waterproof trench coat; and in addition my Mass kit strapped on my back, on the off chance that some days at least I may be able to offer the Holy Sacrifice on the spot where so many men have fallen.

As I marched through the ruins of Ypres at the head of the column, an officer ran across the road and stopped me: 'Are you a Catholic priest?' he asked. 'I should like to go to Confession.' There and then, by the side of the road while the men marched by, he made his peace with God, and went away, let us hope, as happy as I felt at that moment. It was a trivial incident, but it brought home vividly to me what a priest was and the wondrous power given him by God.

All the time we were pushing on steadily towards our goal across the battlefield of the previous week. Five days almost continuous rain had made the torn ground worse than any ploughed field, but none seemed to care as so far not a shot had fallen near. We were congratulating ourselves on our good luck, when suddenly the storm burst. Away along the front trenches we saw the S.O.S. signal shot into the air, two red and two green rockets, telling the artillery behind of an attack and calling for support. There was little need to send any signal as the enemy's guns had opened fire with a crash, and in a moment pandemonium, like fifty first-class thunderstorms, were set loose.

On we hurried in the hope of reaching cover, when right before us the enemy started to put down a heavy barrage, literally a curtain of shells, to prevent reinforcements coming up. There was no getting through that alive and, to make matters worse, the barrage was creeping nearer and nearer, only fifty yards away, while shell fragments hummed uncomfortably close. Old shell-holes there were in abundance, but every one of them was full of water, and one would only float on top. Here was a fix! Yet somehow I felt that though the boat seemed in a bad way, the Master was watching even while he seemed to sleep, and help would surely come.

In the darkness I stumbled across a huge shell crater, recently made, with no water. Into it we rolled and lay on our faces, while the tempest howled around and angry shells hissed overhead and burst on every side. For a few moments I shivered with fear, for we were now right in the middle of the barrage and the danger was very great, but my courage came back when I remembered how easily He who had raised the tempest saved His Apostles from it, and I never doubted He would do the same for us. Not a man was touched, though one had his rifle smashed to bits.

We reached Headquarters, a strong blockhouse made of concrete and iron rails, a masterpiece of German cleverness. From time to time all during the night the enemy gunners kept firing at our shelter, having the range of it to a nicety. Scores exploded within a few feet of it, shaking us till our bones rattled; a few went smash against the walls and roof, and one burst at the entrance nearly blowing us over, but doing no harm thanks to the scientific construction of the passage. I tried to get a few winks of sleep on a stool, there was no room to lie down with sixteen men in a small hut. And I came to the conclusion that so far we had not done badly and there was every promise of an exciting time.

6 August. The following morning, though the Colonel and other officers pressed me very much to remain with them on the ground that I would be more comfortable, I felt I could do better work at the advanced dressing-station, or rather aid-post, and went and joined

the doctor. It was a providential step, as the following night a shell again burst at the entrance to the block-house, but this time exploded several boxes of rockets which had been left at the door. A mass of flame and dense smoke rushed into the dugout, severely burning some and almost suffocating all the officers and men with poisonous fumes before they made their escape.

Our aid-post was a rough tin shed beside a concrete dugout we christened the Pig Sty. You could just crawl in on hands and knees to the solitary chamber which served as dressing room, recreation hall, sleeping apartment and anything else you cared to use it for. On the floor were some wood-shavings, kept well moistened in dampy weather by a steady drip from the ceiling, and which gave covert to a host of curious little creatures, all most friendly and affectionate. There was room for three but as a rule we slept six or seven officers side by side.

I spent a good part of the day, when not occupied with the wounded, wandering round the battlefield with a spade to bury stray dead. Though there was not very much infantry fighting owing to the state of the ground, not for a moment did the artillery duel cease, reaching at times a pitch of unimaginable intensity. I have been through some hot stuff at Loos, and the Somme was warm enough for most of us, but neither of them could compare to the fierceness of the German fire here. We once counted fifty shells, big chaps too, whizzing over our little nest in sixty seconds, not counting those that burst close by . . .

7 August . . . Word reached me about midnight that a party of men had been caught by shellfire nearly a mile away. I dashed off in the darkness, this time hugging my helmet as the enemy was firing gas shells. A moment's pause to absolve a couple of dying men, and then I reached the group of smashed and bleeding bodies, most

of them still breathing. The first thing I saw almost unnerved me; a young soldier lying on his back, his hands and face a mass of blue phosphorus flame, smoking horribly in the darkness. He was the first victim I had seen of the new gas the Germans are using, a fresh horror of this awful war. The poor lad recognised me, I anointed him on a little spot of unburnt flesh, not a little nervously as the place was reeking with gas, gave him a drink which he begged for so earnestly, and then hastened to the others.

Back again to the aid-post for stretchers and help to carry in the wounded, while all the time the shells are coming down like hail. Good God! how can any human thing live in this? As I hurry back I hear that two men have been hit twenty yards away. I am with them in a moment, splashing through mud and water. A quick absolution and the last rites of the Church. A flash from a gun shows me that the poor boy in my arms is my own servant, or rather one who took the place of my orderly while he was away, a wonderfully good and pious lad.

By the time we reached the first party, all were dead, most of them with charred hands and faces. Little rest that night, for the Germans simply pelted us with gas shells of every description, which, however, thanks to our new helmets did no harm . . .

8 August . . . When night fell, I made my way up to a part of the Line which could not be approached in daylight, to bury an officer and some men. A couple of grimy, unwashed figures emerged from the bowels of the earth to help me, but first knelt down and asked for Absolution. They then leisurely set to work to fill in the grave. 'Hurry up, boys,' I said, 'I don't want to have to bury you as well,' for the spot was a hot one. They both stopped working, much to my disgust, for I was just longing to get away. 'Begobs, Father,' replied one, 'I

haven't the divil a bit of fear in me now after the holy Absolution.' 'Nor I,' chimed in the other, 'I am as happy as a king.' The poor Padre who had been keeping his eye on a row of 'crumps' which were coming unpleasantly near felt anything but happy; however there was nothing for it but to stick it out as the men were in a pious mood; and he escaped at last, grateful that he was not asked to say the rosary . . .

10 August. A sad morning as casualties were heavy and many men came in dreadfully wounded. One man was the bravest I ever met. He was in dreadful agony, for both legs had been blown off at the knee. But never a complaint fell from his lips, even while they dressed his wounds, and he tried to make light of his injuries. 'Thank God, Father,' he said, 'I am able to stick it out to the end. Is it not all for little Belgium.' The Extreme Unction, as I have noticed time and again, eased his bodily pain. 'I am much better now and easier, God bless you,' he said, as I left him to attend a dying man.

The man opened his eyes as I knelt beside him: 'Ah! Father Doyle, Father Doyle,' he whispered faintly, and then motioned me to bend lower as if he had some message to give. As I did so, he put his two arms round my neck and kissed me. It was all the poor fellow could do to show his gratitude that he had not been left to die alone and that he would have the consolation of receiving the Last Sacraments before he went to God.

Sitting a little way off I saw a hideous bleeding object, a man with his face smashed by a shell, with one if not both eyes torn out. He raised his head as I spoke. 'Is that the priest? Thank God, I am all right now.' I took his blood-covered hands in mine as I searched his face for some whole spot on which to anoint him. I think I know better now why Pilate said 'Behold the Man' when he showed our Lord to the people . . .

That night we moved headquarters and aid-post to a more advanced position, a strong concrete emplacement, but a splendid target for the German gunners. For the forty-eight hours we were there they hammered us almost constantly day and night till I thought our last hour had come. There we lived with a foot, sometimes more, of water on the floor, pretty well soaked through, for it was raining hard at times. Sleep was almost impossible—fifty shells a minute made some noise—and to venture out without necessity was foolishness. We were well provided with tinned food, and a spirit lamp for making hot tea, so that we were not too badly off, and rather enjoyed hearing the German shells hopping off the roof or bursting on the walls of their own strong fort.

11 August. [Doyle's last diary entry] I had finished breakfast and had ventured a bit down the trench to find a spot to bury some bodies left lying there. I had reached a sheltered corner, when I heard the scream of a shell coming towards me rapidly, and judging by the sound straight for the spot where I stood. Instinctively I crouched down, and well I did so, for the shell whizzed past my head—I felt my hair blown about by the hot air—and burst in front of me with a deafening crash.

It seemed to me as if a heavy wooden hammer had hit me on the top of the head, and I reeled like a drunken man, my ears ringing with the explosion. For a moment I stood wondering how many pieces of shrapnel had hit me, or how many legs and arms I had left, and then dashed through the thick smoke to save myself from being buried alive by the shower of falling clay which was rapidly covering me. I hardly know how I reached the dugout, for I was speechless and so badly shaken that it was only by a tremendous effort that I was able to prevent myself from collapsing utterly as I had seen so many do from shell shock.

Then a strange thing happened. Something seemed to whisper in my ear, one of those sudden thoughts which flash through the mind: 'Did not that shell come from the hand of God? He willed it should be so. Is it not proof that He can protect you no matter what the danger?' The thought that it was all God's doing acted like a tonic; my nerves calmed down, and shortly after I was out again to see could I meet another iron friend.

As a matter of fact I wanted to see exactly what had happened, for the report of a high explosive shell is so terrific that one is apt to exaggerate distances. An officer recently assured me he was only one foot from a bursting shell, when in reality he was a good 40 yards away. You may perhaps find it hard to believe, as I do myself, what I saw. I had been standing by a trellis-work of thin sticks. By stretching out my hand I could have touched the screen—and *the shell fell smashing the woodwork!* My escape last year at Loos was wonderful, but then I was some yards away, and partly protected by a bend in the trench. Here the shell fell, I might say, at my very feet; there was no bank, no protection except the wall of your good prayers and the protecting arm of God.

That night we were relieved, or rather it was early morning, 4.30 a.m., when the last company marched out. I went with them so that I might leave no casualties behind. We hurried over the open as fast as we could, floundering in the thick mud, tripping over wire in the darkness, and, I hope, some of the lay members cursing the German gunners for disturbing us by an odd shot.

We had nearly reached the road, not knowing it was a marked spot, when like a hurricane a shower of shells came smashing down upon us. We were fairly caught and for once I almost lost hope of getting through in safety. For five minutes or more we pushed on in desperation; we could not stop to take shelter, for dawn was breaking and we should have been seen by the enemy. Right and left, in front and behind, some far away, many very close, the shells kept falling. Crash! One has pitched in the middle of the line, wounding five men, none of them seriously. Surely God is good to us, for it seems impossible a single man will escape unhurt, and then when the end seemed at hand, our batteries opened fire with a roar to support an attack that was beginning. The German guns ceased like magic, or turned their attention elsewhere, and we scrambled on to the road and reached home without further loss.

Doyle's diary-based letter, sent home on 14 August, ends with what proved to be his last message to his father:

I have told you all my escapes, dearest Father, because I think what I have written will give you the same confidence which I feel, that my old armchair up in Heaven is not ready yet, and I do not want you to be uneasy about me. I am all the better for these couple of days' rest, and am quite on my fighting legs again. Leave will be possible very shortly, I think, so I shall only say au revoir in view of an early meeting. Heaps of love to every dear one. As ever, dearest Father, your loving son, Willie.

On 16 August the Allied offensive resumed all along the line. The two Irish Divisions—the 16th (Nationalist) and 36th (Ulster)—which had already suffered heavy losses while holding the line, attacked over undulating farmlands dominated by German blockhouses. Of that engagement, 'black in tragedy', Sir Philip Gibbs, a war correspondent at the time, later wrote:

In spite of their dreadful losses the survivors in the Irish battalions went forward to the assault with desperate valour on the morning of August 16th, surrounded the 'pill-boxes', stormed them through blasts of machine gun fire, and towards the end of the day small bodies of these men had gained a footing on the objectives which they had been asked to capture, but were then too weak to resist German counter-attacks. The 7th and 8th Royal Irish Fusiliers had been almost exterminated, the 9th Dublins lost 15 officers out of 17, and 66 per cent of their men. The two Irish Divisions were broken to bits, and their Brigadiers called it murder. They were violent in their denunciation of the 5th Army for having put their men into the attack after those thirteen days of heavy shelling . . .

There was one figure who had stood out amid the scenes of carnage, that of Father Doyle. 'All through the worst hours he went forward and back over the battlefield with bullets whining about him, seeking out the dying and kneeling in the mud beside them to give them Absolution,' wrote the *Morning Post*'s correspondent. 'His familiar figure was seen and welcomed by hundreds of Irishmen who lay in that bloody place, walking with death with a smile on his face, watched by his men with reverence and a kind of awe until a shell burst near him and he was killed.'

Few authentic details were forthcoming after the battle. Lieut.-Colonel H. R. Stirke, commanding the 8th Dublins, testified that 'he had been sent back by the O.C. of one of the regiments, together with some other non-combatants, as the fighting was very severe and it was not necessary to risk more lives. He remained behind a few hours and then returned to the firing line, like the brave man he was.' Private McInespie, who was acting as his 'runner', claimed to be an eye-witness of his death. Learning that a wounded officer or soldier was lying out in an exposed position, Doyle went out to minister to him. The bombardment and barrage increasing in violence, he started to retire. He had just come up with three officers when a shell fell among them, killing them instantaneously.

General Hickie (who, in a letter of condolence to Doyle's father, described him as 'the most wonderful character that I have ever known') wrote: 'On the day of his death, he had worked in the front line, and even in front of that line, and appeared to know no fatigue—he never knew fear. He was killed by a shell towards the close of the day, and was buried on the Frezenberg Ridge. He was recommended for the Victoria Cross by his Commanding Officer, by his Brigadier, and by myself. Superior Authority, however, has not granted it.' (O'Rahilly's observation was that 'the triple disqualification of being an Irishman, a Catholic and a Jesuit, proved insuperable'.)

Among the many tributes quoted in the biography, one, by a Belfast Orangeman, stands out as having a topical bearing on the 'God on our side' issue of this book: an issue rarely more tragically contested than in the sectarian confrontation in Ulster today. For all his dogmatism, his obsessive urge to emulate the saints and martyrs of old, and his unshakeable belief that the Roman Catholic Church was the only true church, Doyle was no bigot. To men of any belief, there was nothing forbidding or pretentious about his 'saintliness'. Few padres can have given Christianity such a good name.

The Ulster rifleman's tribute was published in the *Glasgow Weekly News* of 1 September 1917:

Father Doyle was a good deal among us. We couldn't possibly agree with his religious opinions, but we simply worshipped him for other things. He didn't know the meaning of fear, and he didn't know what bigotry was. He was as ready to risk his life to take a drop of water to a wounded Ulsterman as to assist men of his own faith and regiment. If he risked his life looking after Ulster Protestant soldiers once, he did it a hundred times in his last few days. The Ulstermen felt his loss more keenly than anybody, and none were readier to show their marks of respect to the dead hero priest than were our Ulster Presbyterians. Father Doyle was a true Christian in every sense of the word, and a credit to any religious faith . . .

No trace of a grave was ever found on the battlefield. 'It seems that the remains of him who so often risked his life to bury friend and foe, lie, commingled with those of countless unnamed companions, beneath the plain of Ypres,' wrote O'Rahilly. He ends his biography by quoting a passage from Doyle's last letter to his father, a passage interpolated among the diary entries. Untypical in its muted allusions to spiritual things, it reads like an expression of purely human grief, wrung out of him by the pity of war.

My poor brave boys! They are lying now out on the battlefield; some in a little grave dug and blessed by their chaplain, who loves them as if they were his own children; others stiff and stark with staring eyes, hidden in a shell-hole where they had crept to die; while perhaps in some far-off thatched cabin an anxious mother sits listening for the well-known step and voice which will never gladden her ear again. Do you wonder in spite of the joy that fills my heart that many a time the tears gather in my eyes, as I think of those who are gone?

CHAPTER SEVEN

GOD ON
BOTH SIDES

LOOKING BACK MORE than 60 years to his service as a young officer on the Western Front, H. E. L. Mellesh summed up the attitude towards religion of his contemporaries in his memoir, *Schoolboy Into War* (published in 1978):

> Church parades we had accepted, they were part of the routine; but those canting clergymen at home, who saw oversimply the Germans as the devil and our cause as God's own, we despised. We quoted with approval J. C. Squire's rhyme:
> God heard the embattled nations sing and shout—
> 'God strafe England'—'God save the King'—
> 'God this'—'God that'—and 'God the other thing.'
> 'My God,' said God, 'I've got my work cut out.'
> That the Germans should have believed, equally with ourselves, that God was on their side, may have surprised us, but it did not shock us. We knew that the German had been a brave enemy and almost always a clean and fair fighter. He had been merely misled by his rulers, his philosophers, his Kaiser. The German soldier was as entitled to fight for his side as were we . . .

This concluding chapter is devoted to the views of soldiers on both sides of no-man's-land, as recorded in two long-forgotten books, *The Army and Religion* (published in 1919) and *German Students' War Letters* (1929). Though the latter can scarcely be taken as representative of the German Army as a whole, a comparison of the two at least points up the sting of Squire's much-quoted verse.

The Army and Religion was compiled by an interdenominational committee of 26 leading churchmen and laymen, and was based on a questionnaire circulated around the army. Three questions were posed. What are the men thinking about religion, morality and society? Has the war made men more open to a religious appeal or has it created new difficulties for belief? What proportion of the men are vitally connected to any of the churches, and what do they think of the churches?

During the last two years of the war some 300 memoranda in answer to the questionnaire were received for analysis by the committee from representative groups and individuals (including officers, privates, padres, doctors and nurses). To the average soldier (had he bothered to read it) the 444 pages of the report would have come as no surprise. To most churchmen it must have suggested that for long they had been living in a fool's paradise. Churchgoing before the war had been mostly lip service. A majority of soldiers (representative of the country as a whole) were in almost total ignorance of what the Christian faith stood for. Hope for a religious revival was so much pie in the sky.

The statistical conclusion of the committee was that only about 20 per cent of soldiers had any 'vital connection' with any of the churches, which were widely regarded as being completely out of touch with reality. The state-endowed Church of England, in particular, stood condemned as autocratic and élitist, its clergy showing little interest in social problems and themselves enjoying a higher standard of living than most. Any respect accorded to Anglican padres was in no way connected with their professional status. It was personality alone that counted.

Despite all this there was abundant evidence that the average soldier was far from being godless. 'The soldier has got religion, but not Christianity', wrote one officer. It was a conclusion that the committee appears to have clutched at with avidity, as some hope for the future, in its introductory remarks:

> Broadly speaking the evidence shows conclusively that at the Front the impact of danger awakens the religious consciousness even of the most unlikely men. It is very remarkable that the whole materialism and anti-religious propaganda, which made so much noise, and apparently had so much vogue among our labouring classes a few years ago seems to have simply withered away in the fire of the Line. The men of the British armies, however dim their faith may be, do in the hour of danger, at least, believe in God, 'the great and terrible God'. Most men we are told pray before they go over the parapet or advance in the face of machine guns, and they thank God when they have come through the battle. It is possible to make too much and too little of this. Granting that it is at best a very elementary form of religion, and that it is usually evanescent enough, it is none the less very significant . . .

Despite conceding that their field of enquiry is 'too vast for generalisation', the committee, deliberating under the chairmanship of the Bishop of Winchester (the Rt. Rev. E. S. Talbot), is prone to pontificating. It is in the raw material of the 'memoranda', scattered about amid the verbiage, that one must look for clearer insights. Though necessarily personalised, the opinions expressed have a good deal in common, as the following extracts indicate:

An officer of a Highland regiment: 'War has not made men *think* more deeply. On the contrary it has made them place thinking below emotion and instinct. The war seems to have revived something ancestral in these men —something elementally religious. This has made it even more impossible for them to harbour the old popular version of Christianity but renders them far more open to vital religion. The appeal must be chivalrous, spiritual, possessed of a driving emotion . . .

'The war has undoubtedly widened the gulf between the men and the churches. They think the latter utterly divorced from real life. The great fact which has been burned into my mind is that, while almost every man goes through times of intense religious emotion in the trenches, very few seem to have the faintest conception that the emotion which has gripped them has anything to do with Christianity. This is a terrible indictment of the Church. The *religious* men whom I have met in the army have been almost entirely men with a strong point of view of their own, usually unorthodox and reformatory . . .'

A New Zealand private: 'The manner of life of a soldier in a camp, surrounded by all the most subtle temptations and hardly a voice raised against them, save for chaplains (who mix with officers when not on church parade), or in the trenches where they are out to slaughter the enemy, create an atmosphere of sordid existence that has not an atom of faith or belief in the ideal life preached by religion.

'On the battlefield material and physical force are so conspicuously predominant that it is easy to suppose that the side with the best equipment will win . . . Under such conditions the reality and power of God are difficult to realise and only the ear of a devout Christian can hear the still, small voice above the roar of the cannon.'

A nurse: 'The majority of men think very little of religion, if they think at all it is something for the trenches, and not to be bothered about at any other time. They apparently take a very materialistic view of life, the majority of them having been brought up to work hard for a living, and that seems to be their chief anxiety . . .'

A 'lady hut worker in one of the great bases in France': 'In practice the Tommies shine in patience, consideration for other people, in courage to the point of insouciance (they *do* "put their troubles in the old kit-bag"). But they break down under temptation to drink and other forms of vice and they lack courage to stand out against a crowd. Their idea of a Christian man is that he must not drink, must not gamble and must not amuse himself: on the positive duties, he *must* go to church . . .'

A padre: 'Nothing is so strong in sway over the soul of British soldiers as *what others think*. Nothing is stronger than the reluctance to set yourself up to be better than others. Army life fosters the herd instinct, the sticking-together frame of mind. I was struck the other day when I picked up a driver who had been stunned by a fall from a horse. As he struggled back to a muddled consciousness he muttered—"Eh, but the lads will laff at me for this" . . .'

A padre: 'The only men out here with the capacity for independent thought are the Colonials. Their continual observation of Englishmen is that they have no initiative, which, of course, can only spring from independent thought . . . War reveals the Englishman as the best-hearted, the most enduring and most ignorant and least original man in the world. The work of the Church is to help him to build up what he has not got on the basis of what he has.'

A Colonel in command of a labour unit: '. . . A more cheerful, willing, unselfish lot of men I never hope to see.

Working right up to the front they are perfectly happy, sing all day, and always have a smile or a joke. Only those who have been out here at the front know the HALO that surrounds the simplest British soldier. All the peevishness and selfishness and churliness of people seem burnt clean away. And with all this there is an indescribable boyishness of mind and of understanding that makes them the most lovable people on God's earth. They sing their silly little songs and make their feeble little jokes and have not the faintest idea what splendid souls they are, and therein lies their charm. They may not yet have entered the Kingdom of Heaven, but when they do, it will be as a little child.'

An artillery major: 'It was a wet cold morning, about 6 a.m. in the winter, on the Somme. I saw half a dozen of my boys taking charge of two infantrymen at their last gasp from mud, wet and exposure. The poor fellows had actually laid down to die at the roadside by our battery. My men gave them their breakfast (we were short of rations at the time), their socks (we were short of these), shirts and everything, and rubbed them and lit fires all round them, and sweated over them, and got them to hospital. Now, they would be utterly surprised to hear that any of this had to do with morality or religion. Morality and religion have to do with not breaking laws . . .'

An infantry officer: '. . . As a junior officer, let me say one word for the men. Our British Tommy is just wonderful—a hero! Courage, determination and cheerful endurance are all just part of him. Warm-hearted generosity and cheerful obedience are written all over him. We officers are proud of our lads and some day we may even allow ourselves to say, "We loved them." . . .'

A padre: 'I am increasingly and incessantly astounded at the qualities of our men. How they can go on, as so many have, for 3 years, practically, with only 4 days at home during that time, under the conditions we have to face out here, and yet remain so unchangingly cheerful and ready to do and face anything, is something one could never have imagined in peace-time . . . Unredeemed human nature is infinitely nobler than I had dreamed . . .'

An infantry officer (on belief in a life after death): 'The young have a vague instinct that somehow, somewhere, life *as we know it*, goes on. There is hardly the shadow of a semblance to any Christian doctrine, because there is no hint of a conception of sin, or of life as a tainted thing crying for purification . . .'

An RAMC captain: 'The life beyond the grave is very widely believed in, though in a vague way. It is apparently taken for granted by many that all "good fellows" who die for their country will go to Heaven, but that there is a future judgement for the cruel, and specially for the German War Lords . . .'

A New Zealand private: 'I don't think many pay much consideration to the life beyond death. It is all death here, and life is pretty miserable . . .'

For members of the committee it must have been hard to reconcile those glowing testimonials to the qualities of the Tommy in the trenches with the other side to his nature as revealed in rest periods. One can sense Victorian-nurtured hackles rising as they ponder the overwhelming evidence of widespread drunkenness, gambling, 'foul, immoral blasphemous language', and, most heinous vice of all, 'impurity'. The red lamps of the Army-condoned brothels glimmer from the pages of the report almost like a reflection of hell-fire.

'It is perfectly clear that the excessive use of drink is one of the chief causes of that which is by far the darkest stain, the prevalence of sexual immorality,' proclaims the committee. 'That is the darkest and most tragic element in this chapter, and clearly also the greatest evil among our men. There is probably more about it in the papers we have received than about all the other evils put together.'

An Anglican padre minces no words in his memorandum.

No one who has lived the life of a soldier in France can doubt that impurity is the greatest problem the churches have to face. Many fine lads have ruined themselves through self-indulgence in this direction. For months together the men are in places where it is impossible to get hold of women-folk, then they are drafted within reach of places where there are red lamp houses officially constituted and many houses not so constituted.

The padre goes on to suggest an evil even more insidious than drink as the root of the problem.

To tell a young lad that it is naughty to say 'damn', it is wicked to go to the theatre and not to arm him against self-abuse is a crime. For the church to sit tight because the problem is a delicate one or to excuse herself by saying it is a father's duty is shameful. A young man who has indulged himself secretly for years is comparatively helpless in face of the temptation which faces a man in France. This is the greatest moral problem of all.

That the committee did not entirely close its mind to more tolerant attitudes towards the temptations of the flesh is indicated by their inclusion of comments by two other padres, nonconformist and Anglican, who might almost appear to be in sympathy with the Tommy. The nonconformist padre, serving in Salonika, writes:

The moral weaknesses of the men are inevitable almost (owing to conditions of life etc.). The men in Gallipoli had an intelligible craving for pickles. The virile body

craves excitement, titillation, and because the temptations are so strong and so intelligible to everyone in the
army, surrender to them is condoned. Sins of the body
are not felt to be disgraceful. The cheeriest bunch of men I
ever met perhaps were patients in a venereal hospital at
Marseilles.

The Anglican's brief comment seems to come from the
heart:

One man said to me that the most glorious moment in all
his experience was when he woke to consciousness in a
base hospital and saw the face and smile of a woman and
heard her voice, and the rustle of her skirt. I can quite
understand him.

What is sadly lacking from this worthy, garrulous and
often naïve report is the voice of the Tommy himself. It is
rather like hearing a case presented, and judgement passed, in
front of an empty witness-box. That the committee may
themselves have been aware of this is indicated by the
exceptional space they allow for one memorandum which
has little bearing on the questionnaire, makes no reference to
religion or morality, but which gives flesh and blood to one
soldier, at a given time, in a given place.

The writer was a private in the RAMC. A non-combatant
he writes about what would be regarded at the front as a
non-event. It is a simple account of a routine occasion which
innumerable Tommies must have experienced. Nothing
much happens. There are no soul-searching reflections. But,
between the lines, one seems to get close to the heart of the
matter: into the mind of an individual soldier, temporarily
cut off from the comforting camaraderie of his fellows, alone
with himself—and perhaps his God.

A chap is frightened to think, for it makes him wretched
—the thought of what he might have been doing at home

now—out with the girl, at the pictures or the theatre etc. The job one dreads is to be on guard all night, to stand alone for hours in a shelled village behind the line with the atmosphere of death and destruction around him— ruined houses—a shattered church tower standing ghast- ly in the dull moonlight—the grey darkness softened by the star shells over the line a short distance away—the rattle of musketry, an occasional boom of a gun several miles behind, the spitting of a machine gun—contrasted with the awful silence of the deserted village itself, broken by the fall of a slate as a stray bullet 'pings' on the roof of a ruin—the scuttling of hundreds of rats, the hum of mosquitoes, and the slow silent tread of the men going to and from the line with rations, ammunition, relief parties.

Then the tread of the stretcher bearers, with their burden shrouded in a blanket, on their way to the ambu- lance aid-post in a cellar of the old village—the groan of the wounded man as he passes; and then occasionally a burying party—the spade work in the little meadow, the smothered voices, the little crosses in the darkness, the muffled tread of the grave diggers on their way to their cellar-billet where they will drown the remembrance of their night's work in a good rum ration, and tumble into 'bed'—a blanket on the floor—to sleep till the following day.

And again, nothing but the silence of the village —silence pungent with the scent of roses and flowers growing uncared for in the little garden which 3 years ago was the pride of happy, simple country people and the play-ground of little children; a broken crucifix at the cross-roads, a shrine with remnants of little 'gifts' placed there by children's hands.

Dawn—'stand to' in the line—machine guns more active—more big guns begin to speak—Fritz strafes the old village again with half a dozen shells just to remind the ruins that he is still near. An aeroplane hums some-where overhead—and to the unspeakable joy of the man on guard 'kindly light' supersedes the darkness. Soon he is relieved by his pal who 'comes on next', and, after a swig of rum, he goes to sleep in his clothes. He may remark during the course of the day, 'It was a hell of a night—there ought to be two for company'. He has been forced to think.

In a Germany heading towards a dictatorship in which the Führer would take upon himself the attributes of God and the Church become a lackey of the Fatherland, a publication like *The Army and Religion* would have been an anachronism. For the first time in its history the German Army marched into the Second World War without the blessing of the Church.

Very different was the attitude at the start of the First World War. At a mass rally in Berlin the Kaiser himself delivered the kind of prayer that was rising to heaven from many a pulpit and parade ground in Britain:

Almighty and merciful God, Lord of Hosts, in all humil-ity we beg Thy mighty support for our German Father-land. Bless the whole German Army. Lead us to victory and grant us grace to prove ourselves as Christians always in the face of our enemies. May we soon attain to a peace which will guarantee the honour and independence of Germany.

In the German edition of *German Students' War Letters*, the reliance of God expressed in a number of the 20,000 letters collected from the relatives of the young officers who wrote them (all killed during the war), must have been anathema to the growing cohorts of Nazis. But at least they were offset by the fervour with which the Fatherland was so frequently invoked, not infrequently as a super-race.

The selection from these letters translated and arranged by
A. F. Wedd in 1929 came at a time when a spate of books
were depicting for the first time the horrors rather than the
heroics of the war (notably, in England, the memoirs of
Sassoon, Graves and Blunden). Wedd's sympathetic introduction mirrors the prevailing mood. Only from hindsight
can its chilling implications be seen.

. . . Many English people have been accustomed to think
of the German Army as a horde, if not of actual barbar-
ians, yet of primitive, unreasoning automatons, blindly
obeying the orders of the slave-drivers with whips and
revolvers. Many of those who volunteered during the
war had escaped the brutalising influence of the 'blood
and iron' militarism which prevailed under the old sys-
tem. Thoughtful, poetic, romantic, religious youths for
the most part, they hate war in itself and shrink from the
bloodshed, the dirt, the terror and the privations; yet to
not one of them is there any question of where their duty
lies; the Fatherland has need of its sons and as a matter of
course they must answer the call. The writers look
forward to a regeneration of their country and ultimately
of the world, through their sufferings . . .

These letters apply only to a minority of the German
Army, young men likely to have been brought up in God-
fearing middle-class families. It is significant that among the
German soldiers pictured in Remarque's classic *All Quiet on
the Western Front*, religion apparently means as little as for the
British Tommy. What does emerge from the letters is a
current of religious and patriotic fervour rarely encountered
in the letters of young British officers that have survived.

It may here be appropriate to quote one of the few references to young officers in *The Army and Religion*. Written by
a Royal Flying Corps officer, it strangely appears without
comment. One might have imagined that the committee

(which included the headmaster of Rugby School among its members) would have had reservations about its findings. One can scarcely credit, for example, that the average public school officer, subjected throughout his boyhood to a daily dose of school chapel Christianity, would have been in such ignorance as is suggested.

The average young officer has no philosophy of life at all. He thinks the Christian revelation 'damned nonsense', though he has not the courage to say so. During six months at morning masses held 3 times a week, the highest attendance was 3 officers. Most are entirely ignorant of the elementary facts of Christianity. The religion at his home and school was a vague, indefinite belief in a vague, indefinite God who must never be mentioned.

The bulk of the young German officers' letters were written in the early part of the war, and there is no telling how their faith would have withstood prolonged service in the trenches. In one of the later letters, in November 1916, a theology student was writing, 'Death is the only conqueror. We are all disillusioned.' In the extracts that follow belief is still strong, the suffering bearable in the cause of God and the Fatherland.

Benno Ziegler, aged 22, medical student: September 1914. If only the hand of God, who up till now has graciously led me unscathed through all fatigues and dangers, continues to protect me, it shall not be my fault if I too am not a Man when I come home. I am counting more than ever on that for truly the war-horror seems to have reached its climax.

O God! how many have those hours been when on every side gruesome Death was reaping his terrible harvest. One sees someone fall—one can't immediately recognise who it is—one turns the blood-covered face up—O God! it's you! Why had it to be just *you*! And how often that happened!

At such moments I had but one picture before my mind's eye. I saw you, my dear, good Father, as you laid your hands in blessing upon my head—beside your bed it was, on the morning when I thought I must go—and you prayed for God's mercy on me. Father! your blessing has helped me! It was that which has made me strong, stronger than my comrades—for there have been times when I have been able to comfort and encourage them —I, the weakling!

Paul Muller, 20, theology student: October 1914. . . . The band outside has just been playing 'Praise the Lord, the mighty King of Glory'. We haven't got as far as that yet, but at any rate we have not lost our belief that in spite of everything God is leading us to a good end— otherwise the sooner we are dead the better . . .

November 1914. I dream so often of you. Then I see our house in the moonlight. In the sitting-room a light is burning. Round the table I see your dear heads. Uncle Lav is reading, Mum is knitting stockings, Dad is smoking his long pipe and holding forth about the war. I know that you are all thinking of me. If only warfare accomplishes the right kind of success: if it brings blessing upon the Fatherland and eventually on the whole of mankind: if we are sure of that we should bear our suffering and privation gladly. How I thank God that I am naturally endowed with such powers of endurance. I never felt so strong as I do now . . .

March 1915. . . . It is painful to die far away from home, without a loving eye to look down upon one. A grave at home surrounded with love, to which loved ones come to weep and pray, is granted to few soldiers. But hush! the Heavenly Father has commanded the Guardian Angel to console the dying; he bends lovingly over him and shows him already the crown, the unfading crown, which awaits him above . . .

Franz Blumenfeld, 24, law student: October 1914. . . . One thing weighs on me more from day to day—the fear of being brutalised. Your wishing you could provide me with a bullet-proof vest is very sweet of you, but strange to say I have no fear, none at all, of bullets and shells, but only of this spiritual loneliness. I am afraid of losing my faith in human nature, in myself, in all that is good in the world! Oh, that is horrible! Much, much harder than anything else for me is to endure the coarse fare that prevails among the men here. What is the good of escaping all the bullets and shells, if my soul is injured! . . .

Karl Aldag, 25, student of philosophy: 11 November 1914. Today at 10 o'clock we had a Parade Service. A village church, which had already served as a Field Hospital and was strewn with straw, was decorated with greenhouse plants and flowers. The Divisional Protestant Chaplain read a passage from the Bible and we sang a hymn ('Follow Me, Christians'). Then came a sermon, followed by the chorale 'Now thank we all our God'. It was a moving ceremony, full of thoughts of home; our minds turned from outward things and were occupied with deep, manly, sorrowful meditation, with religious faith, hope and gratitude. The men often tell one another how much more religious our people have become owing to this war; it is touching to hear the men talk confidentially to us too about this. Scoffers either no longer dare to express their views or else have ceased to exist . . . I thank dear Mother for the little text out of the Psalms: it did me a great deal of good.

18 December. It is a strange kind of Christmas this year: so really contrary to the Gospel of Love—and yet it will be more productive of love than any other—love for

one's own people and love to God. I honestly believe that this year the Feast will make a deeper impression than ever and there will be a blessing to many in spite of the war.

I have been singing our Christmas hymns with great delight and moved by the most devout feelings. We sing them in our rest billet, a big warm cow-house, with, on one table, a little lit-up Christmas tree which somebody has had sent from home. I realised the whole mystery of the Redemption and the miracle of the Incarnation as I never have during a sermon. On Christmas Day I shall be at home in thought all the time, and I cannot do more than wish you a devout, holy Christmas Feast, which will bring trust in the God of love who will protect us all. I have perfect confidence in the future.

Christmas at the Front! We were relieved on the eve of the 23rd about 10. The English had been singing hymns including a fine quartet. On our side too the beautiful old songs resounded, with only now and then a shot between. The sentry-posts in the trenches were decorated with fir-branches and tinsel from home—also the dug-outs. Then at 10 o'clock another company arrived and we marched to billets.

In the evening we had our real Christmas celebration. There were 2 big trees standing all lit up on big tables. We got everything we could possibly wish for—knitted comforts, tobacco, cake, chocolate, oranges. Then the Colonel and the Divisional Chaplain came in. The Bible story of Christmas was read and the dear old hymns were sung . . .

3 January 1915. New Year's Eve was very queer here. An English officer came across with a white flag and asked for a truce from 11 a.m. to 3 p.m. to bury the dead (just before Christmas there were some fearful enemy attacks here in which the English lost many men killed

and prisoners). The truce was granted. It is good not to see the corpses in front of us any more. The truce was moreover extended. The English came out of their trenches into no-man's-land and exchanged cigarettes, tinned meat and photographs with our men, and said they didn't want to shoot any more. So there is an extraordinary hush, which seems quite uncanny. Our men and theirs are standing up on the parapets above the trenches.

Then an English officer came across and said that the Higher Command had given orders to fire on our trenches and that our men must take cover, and the artillery began to fire, certainly with great violence but without inflicting any casualties. In the evening we called across to tell each other the time and agreed to fire a salvo at midnight. It was a cold night. We sang songs, and then clapped (we were only 60–70 yards apart): we played a mouth organ and they sang and we clapped. Then I asked if they hadn't got any musical instrument, and they produced some bagpipes (they are the Scots Guards, with the short petticoats and bare legs) and they played some of their beautiful elegies on them and sang too. Then at 12 we all fired salvoes *into the air!* We had brewed some grog and drank the toast of the Kaiser and the New Year.

Walter Böhm, 21, philosophy student (in a letter asking his mother not to send him amulets and other lucky charms): January 1915. . . . Supernatural means of protection I reject. Do you really think, dear Mother, that the Law of Nature with regard to a bullet is going to be reversed in favour of such an unimportant member of the Universe as I am? I am content if I can die in the consciousness that I have not lived to the disadvantage of anyone, that I have done my duty as a member of human society, and that I have not knowingly injured anybody . . .

George Stiller, 20, commercial student: May 1915. I have performed my Sunday devotions today, a thing I very seldom did in time of peace. One learns to pray again here and to cling to one's dear God. Danger has brought me near to my God again. I believe this has been the experience of many others who also had thoughtlessly forgotten God and their religion but who now, through death and danger, have regained their faith . . . The war has deprived us of so much good that we hold dear, but it will also be productive of much good. After the war there will be a deepening of religious feeling and people will be simple and more devout . . .

Heinz Pohlmann, 20, philosophy student: 25 May 1916. Most tenderly loved parents, When you get this letter I am afraid you will be in great sorrow, because then I shall be no longer in this world. I am going into the battle quite calmly and am not in the least afraid to look death in the face, for I feel myself safe in the Hands of God. Jesus Christ, whom after wandering long astray I was at last graciously brought to acknowledge as my Saviour, is to me too the Resurrection and the Life. Perhaps you do not share my conviction, but I have found some appropriate words in my book by Lhotzkk: 'Many roads lead from men to God, but from God to men only one' . . .

Pohlmann's evident premonition of his death came true: he was killed 7 days later. At the end of his letter he had drawn his parents' attention to two Scriptural texts—Corinthians II, 13.13, and Psalm 43.5. They read 'All the saints salute you' and 'Why art thou cast down, O my soul! and why art thou disquieted within me? hope in God: for I shall yet praise Him who is the health of my countenance, and my God.'

Karl Gorzel, 21, law student: June 1916. . . . The finest thing of all is the marvellous comradeship at the Front. I think that this alone must give us a great pull over the motley crew of enemies facing us. Over there every man must first have to look to see whether the comrade appearing before him is of his own race or not—we could not very well respect a nigger as a comrade . . .

1 October (at Thiepval during the Battle of the Somme). . . . Suddenly the barrage lifts—the shells are falling behind us—and there, close in front, is the first wave of the enemy! Release at last! Every one who is not wounded, every one who can raise an arm, is up, and like a shower of hailstones our bullets pelt upon the attacking foe!

The first wave lies prone in front of our holes, and already the second is upon us, and behind the English are coming on in a dense mass. Anyone who reaches our line is at once polished off in hand-to-hand bayonet fighting, and now our bombs fly with redoubled force into the enemy's ranks. They do their gruesome work there, and like ripe ears of corn before the reaper the English attacking columns fall. Only a few escape in full flight.

We sink down, dazed, upon the tortured earth, and tie up the wounded as well as we can, while awaiting the coming of a second attack or of the night. The machine-guns are buried in soil and smashed by shells: the stock of bombs is almost exhausted: the fire becomes violent again: it makes one's head ache and one's lips burn. The issue now lies in the Hands of God. There is only one thought in every mind: 'They shall not take us alive!'

The question must arise in reading the letters in this unique collection as to how meaningful were some of the more emotive thoughts expressed. From the last two letters quoted one may safely conclude that Karl Gorzel would not have written as he did had he not known that his parents would have been proud of his evident zest for battle, even of his racist outlook (so grimly prophetic of German youth to come). But how much were the expressions of religious fervour in some of the other letters genuinely heartfelt, and how much mere lip service, written to reassure and meet with the approval of pious parents?

Two letters, at least, attest to a solid and lasting faith, written as they were at the very gates of death. 'I am lying on the battlefield', both begin, and one cannot but wonder in what dire circumstances they were scrawled, and how many others like them might have been found when a battle had ebbed, and never since have come to light. What is noticeable in the brief farewells of these two, both theology students, is that their last thoughts were centred on 'home'—an earthly and a heavenly home. There is now no breath of patriotism. The Fatherland no longer counts.

Eduard Bruhn, aged 25, from Kiel, was serving on the Russian front, on 17 September 1915, when the end came:

Dear Parents, I am lying on the battlefield badly wounded. Whether I recover is in God's hands. If I die, do not weep. I am going blissfully home. A hearty greeting to you all once more. May God soon send you peace and grant me a blessed home-coming. Jesus is with me, so it is easy to die. In heartfelt love, Eduard.

The letter from Johannes Haas, aged 19, from Leipzig, is the last of three of his published in the collection. They may fittingly end this book as testifying to a reliance on God beyond the reach of partisan propaganda. It may be noted that in the second of the three letters, written to a friend, Haas makes no reference to religion in his spontaneous outburst at the joys of living. But for his parents he would have left no doubt that there was cause for rejoicing, as well as grief, in his death: that heaven had taken him to his long home and the trumpets had sounded for him on the other side.

13 May 1916. Before Verdun. My dear good old parents, Here we have war, war in its most appalling form, and in our distress we realise the nearness of God. Things are becoming very serious: but I am immensely unalarmed and happy. 'Let me go, I long to see my Jesus so.'

It must be splendid to see God in all His glory and His peace after all that, with human misunderstanding, one has longed and struggled for! I think often and joyfully of the next world. I do not fear the Judgement. I was indeed a poor sinful creature, but how great is God's mercy and the Saviour's love! So, without fear or dismay, I do my duty to the Fatherland and to my dear German people.

I thank you, dear Parents, for having led me to the Saviour; that was the best thing you ever did. I love you tenderly. God be with you! Hans.

28 May. [To a friend] Life is indeed beautiful! Dinner in the Cadets' Mess. Afterwards the musical ones gather round the piano. Beethoven's Sonatas; Chopin's wonderful Ballades, Nocturnes and Waltzes: and Schumann: it is delightful! Then I go out into the sunshine and dream. The day after tomorrow I return to the Front. Don't let's brood about that. Life is worth fighting and running risks for . . .

1 June. Dear Parents, I am lying on the battlefield, wounded in the body. I think I am dying. I am glad to have time to prepare for the heavenly home-coming. Thank you dear Parents. God be with you. Hans.